"I have watched for years as the Lord has blessed Scott Dawson and his ministry. It has been a blessing to see—and to be a part of—his reach throughout the world, partnering with Scott on several occasions and encouraging him in his work. Through the Next Generation Alliance ministry of the Palau team, I have seen firsthand Scott's loyalty to the Gospel, to the church, to the Bible, and to evangelism. His ministry—through initiatives such as Safe at Home—is reaching individuals all over the country.

I wish Scott all the best in the days ahead, and pray the Lord continues to use him in mighty ways, to the glory of the Lord."

Luis Palau, World Evangelist (www.palau.org)

"Scott Dawson has opened my eyes with this culturally relevant guide to evangelism. I read the book in one sitting and learned about the present and future of evangelism and how it should look in our contemporary culture. This relevant material is life-changing."

Pat Williams, senior vice president, Orlando Magic; author, *What Are You Living For?*

"Scott Dawson is on the cutting edge of evangelism. He understands the truths of Scripture and the times in which we live. He understands the need of the hour and tells us how to fix it. Like a good physician, he can diagnose the disease and show us the cure we need in God's Word. We need men like Scott Dawson and Scott Lenning. More importantly, we need to listen to what they say. The times are changing, but the truths are still applicable. The authors' ability to state how we can be more effective in evangelism in the 21st century is a message that should be read by every pastor, staff member and lay person interested in reaching our culture for Christ."

Michael Catt, senior pastor, Sherwood Baptist Church; executive producer, Sherwood Pictures, Albany, Georgia

"'Evangelism is one beggar showing another beggar where he can find a piece of bread.' This definition by D. T. Niles is the best description of evangelism I know, and it undergirds Scott Dawson's approach to this vital ministry of the church. In a culture saturated with showmanship and marketing schemes, Scott reminds us of the

D0858636

nonnegotiable essentials of prayer, integrity, community, and the necessity of a cross-centered message of forgiveness and grace. An encouraging word for all who know Jesus and want to make him known to others."

Timothy George, founding dean of Beeson Divinity School of Samford University; senior editor, *Christianity Today*

"Over the last several years as my relationship with Scott Dawson has grown, I've discovered his passion for the Gospel permeates every aspect of his life. In his new book *Evangelism Today*, he teaches timeless truths of how this generation and generations to come can discover a living relationship with God through Jesus Christ. This book could be the one tool God uses to sharpen you to reach your neighbor, friend, or associate for Christ today."

David Green, founder and CEO, Hobby Lobby

"Scott Dawson's and Scott Lenning's book makes sharing the Good News relevant in a changing society. While reading their book about evangelism today, I was reminded of a recent conversation with key pastors in a major city. The pastors shared that their young people were simply not interested in sharing their faith with their friends. Shocked as I was, I inquired. The response was that tolerance, which has been portrayed to the young people of our society as acceptable, has become the norm. God has called all believers to the Great Commission, to feed the poor and dying. People may think it is rude to confront others with any objective truth today. Yet the Holy Spirit still works. And he has people ready to receive personal input about the Savior, done gently and respectfully. Youth today respect Jesus Christ. They may not see him as a religious figure, but they respect him. What a wonderful opportunity to authentically, intentionally, and creatively share the truth about him in word and deed. Scott Dawson and Scott Lenning's book shares how to communicate him appropriately in a changing society. Our thanks to them and Baker Books for making this volume available to the church."

Tom Phillips, vice president, Crusade Ministries, BGEA

EVANGELISM
TODAY

EVANGELISM TODAY

Effectively Sharing *the* Gospel
in a Rapidly Changing World

SCOTT DAWSON
WITH SCOTT LENNING

BakerBooks

a division of Baker Publishing Group
Grand Rapids, Michigan

Published by Baker Books
a division of Baker Publishing Group
P.O. Box 6287, Grand Rapids, MI 49516-6287
www.bakerbooks.com

Printed in the United States of America

Library of Congress Cataloging-in-Publication Data

Dawson, Scott.
    Evangelism today : effectively sharing the Gospel in a rapidly changing world / Scott Dawson with Scott Lenning ; foreword by Josh McDowell.
       p.   cm.
    Includes bibliographical references.
    ISBN 978-0-8010-7133-1 (pbk.)
    1. Evangelistic work—United States. I. Lenning, Scott. II. Title.
BV3790.D422 2009
269′.2—dc22
                                           2009006193

Published in association with the literary agency of Sanford Communications, Inc., Portland, Oregon, www.sanfordci.com.

In keeping with biblical principles of creation stewardship, Baker Publishing Group advocates the responsible use of our natural resources. As a member of the Green Press Initiative, our company uses recycled paper when possible. The text paper of this book is comprised of 30% post-consumer waste.

To those who live like there is no tomorrow
and who know today must be impacted for Christ.

Contents

ACKNOWLEDGMENTS

Over the last three years this book has been a journey for answers to important questions—questions that are significant both personally and professionally. Where is the future of evangelism? How can we reach a society that is increasingly lending a deaf ear to evangelicals and, even worse, becoming antagonistic to the message of Christ? Throughout this journey there have been those who have stood beside and behind me to accomplish this task.

Like in most works, this book is based entirely on a team. The quarterback, Scott Lenning, led the charge with countless interviews and investigations into what leaders are thinking in the area of evangelism. He is a trusted friend and advisor, and this book was heavy upon his shoulders. The running back was no doubt Kim Beverage. Kim is a new face around our office and joined our team as my assistant just when this book became a pressing deadline. She would not stop until the goal was finished and the project had been completed.

The frontline was made up of the entire Scott Dawson Evangelistic Association. The team of sixteen individuals who come together with a vision of doing something much greater than any one of us could do on our own is what drives us to each new challenge. Gina Handley and Mike Greer took on additional responsibilities so Scott and I could finish this book.

No team can succeed without a good coach. David Sanford and Sanford Communications, Inc., staff made sure the team was working (even when we were exhausted) so the book could be finished. David kept the goal in front of us—not just to be published, but to impact with the gospel those who will never hear Scott Dawson in person. For that, I will always be thankful. Elizabeth Honeycutt is an incredible editor. She encouraged me through the grammatical challenges and strengthened the issues presented in this book. Rebekah Clark and Elizabeth Jones are well on their way to ruling the world!

I also want to thank the board of the ministry. These individuals believe that the message of Christ is still relevant and life changing. Their friendship is unmatched, and their commitment to Christ is thrilling. I wish I could mention each one by name and share with you all of the times they have personally impacted my life, but the word count would put this book in jeopardy of never being published. The sacrifice of these men—along with so many others who have invested financially in this ministry in order for the gospel to go out—is humbling. Thank you for your confidence, which is a constant source of encouragement.

Big thanks to Chad Allen and the rest of the team at Baker for their tenacious spirit for excellence. I appreciate Dan Baker and his ability to always see the big picture for impact.

Finally, a team must have some good cheerleaders! Tarra, my helpmate over the last decade and a half, is the rock. She is Proverbs 31 exemplified every day. Her spirit is gentle, her attitude is positive, and her speech is biblical. My prayer is for my son, Hunter, to find a wife like his mom. Hunter is a great kid who loves baseball only less than he loves his Savior. His insight is at times surprising for a tweenager, but then again he is Tarra's son. Hope is my little angel. She can light up any room with her personality, yet she is also very compassionate. I know God is going to use both of these children in an awesome way to advance his kingdom.

My parents are two of the biggest cheerleaders. They have lived out an example of godly living before me. Throughout my life I have not seen my parents waiver in their faith. They are my heroes. Others who need a shout-out are: Terry and Dottie, who make the best chocolate cake in America at Edgar's Bakery; Tom and Mary Anne, who sent countless meals over for dinner; Dwight and Betty, who are awesome; Pat Northrop, who is like another mom. Phil Drake, David and Barbara Green, C. W., Doug, Danny, Dave, and a host of others who constantly challenge me to be more like Christ tomorrow than I am today. Together let's all commit to share Christ with someone today!

FOREWORD

When I heard another book on evangelism was coming out, I had several thoughts. My first thought pertained to the word itself. *Evangelism* has had several negative connotations over the last decade. People seem to land in one of two camps regarding this word. Some have disdain for it due to past experiences of evangelistic campaigns that had either a warped view of God or a manipulative approach to people. From their personal experience, they have decided that evangelism has lost its significance in the life of the church.

The other side has not heard of the word in a religious sense. They relegate the term *evangelism* to evening newscasts or magazine articles to describe the efforts of secular groups or activists demanding change. These people have never considered themselves evangelists nor have they ever met anyone who demonstrates the true meaning of the word. In both cases there is confusion. Scott Dawson has done a tremendous job of bringing these two camps together. He clearly brings out the distinction of the role of biblical evangelism while not tying the term to the programmatic approach of the past.

The second thought revolved around the change found in evangelism. We cannot continue doing things like we have always done. If this book places us in a "box mentality," it will not serve as a catalyst for change. I am impressed that Scott and his team have taken the time to interview thousands of church leaders to discover not what has been done but what is being dreamed to reach this next generation of leaders.

My third thought was about including the entire body of Christ in the approach of evangelism. If evangelism is presented as an effort in which only a select few can participate, then it is neither biblical nor effective. Evangelism is not about a *program* but about a *person*—Jesus Christ. Evangelism is much more than a *decision*; it is a *life change*. It seems this resource takes the approach that we all are important in advancing the kingdom of God.

Finally, I thought about evangelism and integrity. Who is writing this book? Why would someone write about this topic, and who has the credibility to produce it? Then I learned the author was my good friend Scott Dawson. Over the last decade I have seen Scott mature into one of the greatest leaders of the evangelical community. His style is to engage a culture, not to exclude a generation. He is known as an innovative leader with a desire to see people's lives changed through Christ. You may not know him now, but after you read this book you will have respect and love for his genuine spirit and commitment to Christ.

Over the next few years we will see more change in our country than we have in the past two hundred years. Most people in our communities have not heard of the life-changing power of Jesus Christ. A generation ago Bibles were handed out by community leaders and prayers started each day in our schools. We are now one generation away from the complete secularization of our country with no concept of a personal relationship with Christ. For these reasons, I encourage you to utilize this book to the fullest extent. Use it in your small group, church, or Bible study class and share the passion for evangelism.

Josh D. McDowell, author and speaker

INTRODUCTION

Back to the Basics with a New Twist

Why is there a need for another book on evangelism? That was my question before we began this three-year journey. This project started not as a book but as a personal investigation.

Five years ago I asked my dear friend Scott Lenning to speak at our annual board retreat on the subject "What Is the Future of Evangelism?" His approach was to survey a few friends and see what he could find out. What he discovered became the beginning phase of our quest to find the trends for effective evangelism.

Our concept was simple: interview as many people as we could from all walks of life. We traveled to seminaries, churches, businesses, and parachurches to ask a basic question: "In your opinion, what will it take to be effective in reaching people for Christ in the next ten years?"

It must be noted that we are not necessarily researchers. We did not interview anyone with any other intention than to find out what he or she thought. In addition, we only interviewed those who have a keen interest in evangelism. It made no sense to us, for this project, to interview those who do not pursue the goal of reaching people for Christ.

Over the last three years there have been hundreds of face-to-face conversations and now thousands of emails. Again, this is a pursuit for us to become more effective in what we are already doing. This is not another consultant's attempt to sell a service or program; it is just someone saying that we may not cross the ocean to reach the world, but we can cross the street.

We discovered several common trends in evangelism for the next decade, including the following:

Evangelism must be intentional—our approach in our communities must be thought-out and deliberate.

Evangelism has to be authentic—people need to believe in the person speaking before the message is presented.

Evangelism should be targeted—we are seeing a paradigm shift from *event* to *experience*.

Evangelism must focus on specific groups—students to seniors will seek out those who identify with their struggles and will likely be attracted to people or groups that are similar.

I believe you will be challenged, informed, and inspired by some of the trends presented in this book.

In a world that seems to be attracted to spin, this book is not infallible—neither the authors nor every proposal. This book does not take into account every zip code in our nation or every style in ministry. At times it will seem that the book takes a traditional church position followed by sympathy with the emerging church. It will be both practical and academic, theological and sociological, generic and specific in different parts of the book. In addition, it is assumed that most people surveyed responded based on which aspect they were already involved with in evangelism. Those majoring in prayer responded that it was the most needed, and those working with students said students must be targeted.

My prayer is that reading this book will make you aware of at least three things in our society:

1. The church must recognize that the gospel is still relevant to society. Take the message of salvation out of the church and we are nothing more than another self-help group looking for mutual inspiration to make it through another day. The power of God unto salvation is enough not just to merely survive but to live abundantly!

2. I want you to realize that the church is at a crossroads of belief. I have personally stopped asking individuals *if* they are sharing their faith. I now ask them *why they aren't* sharing their faith. Yes, there are pockets of groups focused on sharing their faith, but those numbers seem either smaller or less known than in previous days. On July 5, 2007, *Christianity Today* asked a panel about the future of mass evangelism. Thirty-eight percent responded that it is no longer effective for our day.[1] Although we must not be unwilling to change methods in being effective, our question is: "What is replacing the preaching to the masses?" It is a serious question, and I am personally concerned by the church's lack of enthusiasm for evangelism.

3. I want you to be aware that God is still working around us. Habakkuk 1:5 says, "Look at the nations, and see! Be astonished! Be astounded! For a work is being done in your days that you would not believe if you were told" (NRSV). I think this is relevant today. God is doing a great work through a businessmen's lunch in Connecticut, a student outreach in Oregon, a women's Bible study in Arizona, and a homeless shelter in Dallas. As smart as we are with iPods, Internet, and instant messaging, we do not grasp the understanding of all God is doing. My challenge for you is to read the following pages and prepare for the days ahead when God does an astonishing work in you and through you.

LOST IN THE SHUFFLE

The Great Commission and American Priorities

It's not about you. The purpose of your life is far greater than your own personal fulfillment, your peace of mind, or even your happiness. It's far greater than your family, your career, or even your wildest dreams and ambitions. If you want to know why you were placed on this planet, you must begin with God. You were born *by* his purpose and *for* his purpose.

—Rick Warren

I am of the opinion that the chief dangers which confront the coming century will be religion without the Holy Spirit, Christianity without Christ, forgiveness without repentance, salvation without regeneration, politics without God and Heaven without Hell.

—William Booth

One of the most fundamental questions of humankind is, "Why am I here?" The day former Beatle George Harrison died, the news report said, "For every human there is a quest to find the answer to why am I here, who am I, where did I come from, where am I going." Harrison himself once said, "For me, that became the most important thing in my life, everything else is secondary." It has plagued our species since the rebellion in the Garden of Eden, and today this question has seeped into the church. Ask any individual in the pew on Sunday morning why the church exists, and you could receive a myriad of answers.

"The church exists to feed the poor," one would say, or another would respond, "To glorify God." Still others would answer, "To disciple believers," and finally some may say, "To win the lost." The answer to this question could be any of these, but the ultimate reason the church exists is to fulfill the Great Commission. "Go therefore and make disciples of all the nations, baptizing them in the name of the Father and of the Son and of the Holy Spirit, teaching them to observe all things I have commanded you; and lo, I am with you always, even to the end of the age" (Matt. 28:19–20 NKJV).

I know some may not agree with my next statement, so I can only ask for it to be read in context of the clarification. After careful review of the interviews and analysis of the three-year journey of this book, I have concluded that unless the church discovers its main purpose in society, in the next thirty years the mammoth cathedrals (megachurches) that are springing up around the country will be reduced to museums or civic halls of the local government.

The church is the only entity not built primarily for its own members. The church stands as a tool of God to be used to effectively reach people's hearts. A quick look on the Internet at the largest churches in America will show quite a different story. *Weight loss, stress management,* and *debt reduction* seem to be the buzzwords on the screen. One can only pray that the gospel message is shared clearly and convincingly within each of these programs.

In Matthew 28:18–20 we realize the important facts of our walk with Jesus Christ. Allow me to share three. First, we see we have a Savior worth serving. Jesus tells his followers that he has been given "all authority on heaven and on earth" (Matt. 28:18). In most circles we frequently discuss the truth that Jesus is all-powerful. Romans 1:16 says, "It is the power of God unto salvation" (NKJV), so evidently Jesus has power. It is one thing to have power, but to have both power and authority—well, that is overwhelming! A three-hundred-pound football player may have power, but he must submit his power to the authority of a referee. A semitruck has all the horsepower it can manage, but it must submit to a police car that has its lights flashing. The use of the term *authority* means that Jesus has the absolute power of heaven and the absolute right here on earth. Therefore, no one can ultimately stand up to his decisions, his commands, or his ways. John Piper states,

> Without this declaration of Jesus' authority, we could never venture confidently to make disciples. On what possible basis do we have any right to tell anybody they should change their whole way of thinking and acting and become a disciple of Jesus Christ? Only one thing could justify such outlandish proselytizing all over the world—that Jesus Christ rose from the dead and has been given an absolute authority over natural and supernatural forces so that every human and every angelic being will give an account to him. If Jesus has that kind of authority, then we Christians not only have the right but are bound by love to tell other people to change and become his disciples.[1]

Second, we discover in Matthew 28 that not only do we have a Savior worth serving but there is also a society worth saving.

As we read in Matthew 28, Jesus tells (commands) his followers to go to "all the nations" (v. 19 NKJV). This command is
associated with the words Luke writes in Acts 1:8 when Jesus
reveals that his disciples will be his "witnesses in Jerusalem,
and in all Judea and Samaria, and to the ends of the earth." It
is noteworthy that this is a geographic approach to missions. It
begins with your closest circle. The growing trend for American
Christianity is to cross the ocean to tell someone about Christ,
but he tells us first to cross the street. This is certainly not true
in every church, but there has been a major increase over the
last decade of churches introducing "short-term" (usually four
to ten days) mission trips. At a recent youth pastors' retreat
sponsored by Scott Dawson Evangelistic Association (SDEA),
thirty youth pastors were surveyed about changes they have
experienced in their youth ministries over the past five years.
This survey revealed that 60 percent of the youth ministries'
summer activities changed from traditional youth camps to
mission trips. Acts 1:8 is addressed to the disciples, and Jerusalem was home to the disciples' closest circle of friends and
family. It is often said that "blood is thicker than water" in
terms of relationships. If so, it seems we should be concerned
with the spiritual welfare of those relationships. Jesus tells us
to go to the ends of the earth, but as we are going we must not
forget to inform the ones we encounter along the way.

Finally, we learn in this passage that we have Scriptures
worth searching. Jesus tells us to teach "all things that I commanded you" (Matt. 28:20 NKJV) as we reach this world for
Christ. This reveals the interconnectedness of true evangelism
and true discipleship. One pastor friend of mine said recently
that it is not hard getting people to trust in a Savior, but it is
difficult to train the new converts to read their Bibles. Another
pastor seemed shocked when the results of his own survey
found that less than a quarter of his congregation read the

Bible on a weekly basis. This is consistent with several studies conducted by the Gallup and Barna organizations. A 2000 Gallup poll found that 37 percent of Americans read the Bible at least once a week, and research from Barna in 1997 reported that those who read the Bible regularly spend about fifty-two minutes a week in the Scriptures.

A major reason most people will not share their faith is ignorance of what they believe. There is a serious problem with Bible study efforts for those of us who say we believe in Jesus as our Savior. It is not known whether this is a current phenomenon or if it is simply that there was no research done for earlier generations. In any case, today's hectic schedule seems to have pushed Bible study time to the sideline. If your life is like mine, we feel compelled to be the best spouse, parent, businessperson, community citizen, and best everything or anything else that jumps into our life. Where is the time for Bible study? Could we be spending too much time attempting to be the best person in the community while sacrificing a personal spiritual transformation in our own life?

When we allow things to get in the way of Bible study, it reduces our confidence in sharing our faith. One businessperson responded, "I feel guilty every time I am in a situation where I can share my faith. I love the Lord, I just do not know enough about him to persuade another person to receive him." You may feel the same way. It is one of the most used tools in Satan's arsenal. Evangelism is not a program we use but a relationship we share. Yes, you should grow in your faith and learn God's Word, but do not wait until you "know it all" before you share this relationship. It is not *what* you know, but *who* you know that is important.

In Luke, Jesus addresses the crowd: "Why do you call me 'Lord, Lord,' and do not do what I say?" (Luke 6:46). If we understand Christ's command to us, there is a case for evangelism to be considered an issue of obedience. The Bible makes it clear that faith comes by hearing the Word of God. "For the word of God is living and active. Sharper than any double-edged sword, it penetrates even to dividing soul and spirit, joints and marrow; it judges the thoughts and attitudes of the heart" (Heb. 4:12). A biblical and relational approach to evangelism always includes a proper use and understanding of the Scriptures. Just like in school, a profession, or a hobby, a Christian should always be improving his or her ability to know, apply, and share Scripture on a consistent basis.

Why Are People Not Receiving Christ?

According to one interview with a leading researcher for the Southern Baptist denomination, their number of conversions today is the same as it was in the 1950s. That sounds fine until you discover that the population in America has now doubled from 149 million in 1950 to over 300 million today. The stagnation of conversions has also impacted church attendance, which has been declining for decades, while the population growth of this country is steadily increasing. If this trend continues, we will soon be losing the equivalent of one church every week. With numbers this staggering, we are compelled to ask what has gone wrong.

Arguably, you could find many different reasons for not accepting Christ depending on geography, economic, or racial boundaries. But there has been a concerted effort by some in the media, educational, and political realms to find and broadcast the major objections to Christianity in America. The reasons uncovered are not intended to be exhaustive, but an overview of what we are facing in our country.

One of the major objections to our faith is the debate over the exclusivity of salvation through Jesus Christ. The consistent response when the gospel is shared has been: "Are you saying that Jesus is the only way to spend eternity in heaven?" In our society of tolerance and plurality, Christians have been moved out of influential circles because of our conviction that salvation is through Jesus's death for the sins of the world. The compelling argument that exists—to think it unfair that God would make salvation so exclusive to one way—causes the answers a Christian must give to seem uncaring, unfair, and ultimately unattractive unless given with a proper response.

Yet people do accept one exclusive rule in many other avenues of daily life. Take football, for example. What if the referees changed the rules and told the teams that they would score touchdowns based on the efforts of the players who scored and when they scored? Or what if the stock exchange altered its guidelines so people could earn and lose income on a wide basis that was judged by a committee? Or what if teachers graded their classes on tests that the students had no way to prepare for in advance? "Unfair" would be the ultimate charge against these ideas.

The accusation that Christianity is unfair to those who have not heard of Christ is usually brought up by a person to whom it does not apply. In addition, it is intended not to help those who have not heard but rather to justify the lifestyle of the individual who asks the question. Like a person told me, "It is not the things I do not know about God that bothers me, but the things I do know about him."

Jesus addresses the crowd in a positive manner when he says, "Let not your heart be troubled; you believe in God, believe also in Me" (John 14:1 NKJV). We still live in a country where a majority of individuals believe in God. Although the numbers have slid a little over the last half century, multiple studies suggest well over three-quarters of the country believe in a personal God. But Jesus does not let us settle for the Hollywood approach to deity: just believe in God and everything will be all right. No, he presses the issue further to explain that there is a need to believe in him exclusively because, as he declares in John 14:6, "I am the way, the truth, and the life. No one comes to the Father except through me." Jesus is the ultimate judge of who gets to the Father. Therefore, as a follower of Jesus Christ, I am bound to follow his instructions. A person may admit that Jesus was a good person, teacher, or philosopher, but that cannot take away his or her sin.

Another element of this particular objection to God's fairness and one way of salvation is the biblical view of God the Father. The Scriptures consistently teach that God is our Father. He is the perfect example of a perfect father. And as a perfect father, he would never allow his only true Son to die the way he did if there was any other way to provide salvation. In a book called *Evangelical Affirmations*, editors Carl Henry and Kenneth Kantzer write, "We affirm that Jesus Christ is fully God and fully man with two distinct natures united in one person. The incarnation, substitutionary death and bodily resurrection of Jesus Christ are essential to the gospel. Through these events a gracious God has acted in time and history to reach out to humanity and save all who believe in Him."[2] If this was Jesus's mission from his Father and there had been any other way to provide salvation, then Christianity would be the most sadistic and pathetic view of life.

Another popular objection to receiving Christ is the hypocrisy within the church organization. It seems every week a Christian leader is accused of an impropriety in the moral, ethical, or professional arena. Newspapers carry the headlines of the failures of those who call themselves Christians. To be blunt, there are hypocrites in the church. One friend of mine tells me we should all wear signs around our necks with the phrase "Under Construction." While it is true that there is hypocrisy in the church, it is not a valid excuse to write off Christianity. When Jesus calls people he never says, "Follow my people." No, Jesus says, "Follow me."

I may have a problem with one experience at Cracker Barrel, but I still love the restaurant. Allow me to explain. One of my favorite places to eat while traveling is Cracker Barrel. There is usually consistent service, food, and availability. But I remember one night, my wife and I stopped at a Cracker Barrel en route to a speaking engagement and had a highly unusual experience. Due to a problem with one of the stoves, we were told our meal would come in stages. Tarra got only green beans and cornbread, while her chicken was delivered five minutes later, followed even later by her other vegetable. I had

Of course, the moment we—or our children—support biblical values in public, we will be accused of intolerance. Tolerance has been so cleverly promoted that when anyone advocates moral values in a community or school, that person is criticized for opposing personal rights. We must understand that personal rights are only valid when moral boundaries exist, because an appeal to "rights" is an appeal to an objective standard of justice, which can only exist in a moral society. Those who denounce moral values (even in the name of tolerance) threaten the very principles to which they appeal. It is no virtue to tolerate behavior that threatens the morality or safety of our children. The Bible makes it clear that "To fear the Lord is to hate evil" (Prov. 8:13).[3]

—Josh D. McDowell, author and speaker

my coffee and grits (yes, I do like them) and waited for sausage and then had eggs for what I guess was dessert. The management apologized but offered no discount on the ticket. Now if this had been my only experience with the restaurant chain, I may have never walked through the door again. But I have eaten at Cracker Barrel restaurants hundreds of times and have always seen a consistent product.

Currently, much attention is given to the failures of some leaders who are Christian—and I am not excusing their actions. But if you look out on a summer evening and see a falling star, it can distract your attention from the constellations that fill the sky on a consistent basis. For every one leader who falls, hundreds of faithful Christians are striving to be a consistent light in a dark atmosphere.

Troubling Trends

Many other objections to receiving Christ include questions concerning the reliability of Scripture and the plurality of religious backgrounds in our country. But there are two reasons for rejecting Jesus Christ that I find especially troubling: (1) An increasing number of Americans simply do not want to follow Jesus. (2) Far too many Americans have never truly been confronted with the gospel of Christ.

Life is pretty good for some, and they don't need or want Jesus. With others a dialogue can continue for months when they are pursuing truth. And even those who are cynical can be convinced. But what about those who have settled for fatalism?

John 3 records a conversation between Jesus and Nicodemus. It is in this context that the most famous verse in the Bible appears—John 3:16. There may have been a time in America when we only needed to quote this verse and people would respond. Hopefully this is still true, but now we must go further along in the text. Jesus gives the ultimate reason people will reject him. It has nothing to do with religions, fairness, or faith; it has to do with their choice to stay within sin.

> For God so loved the world that he gave his one and only Son, that whoever believes in him shall not perish but have eternal life. For God did not send his Son into the world to condemn the world, but to save the world through him. Whoever believes in him is not condemned, but whoever does not believe stands

condemned already because he has not believed in the name of God's one and only Son. This is the verdict: Light has come into the world, but men loved darkness instead of light because their deeds were evil. Everyone who does evil hates the light, and will not come into the light for fear that his deeds will be exposed. But whoever lives by the truth comes into the light, so that it may be seen plainly that what he has done has been done through God.

John 3:16–21

When the gospel is shared and rejected, that rejection is not toward the individual but toward Christ. The Light has come into the world, and some choose to stay in the darkness instead of rushing to the Light. It is so frustrating to know people who are hurting, searching, and ultimately destroying their own life yet not willing to surrender to Christ. The debate will continue concerning God's sovereignty and our choice, but the words of Christ are clear: the ones who do not come to Christ are ultimately rejected because they love their sin more than they would love to be set free.

The second very troubling reason people are not coming to Christ is because they say they have never been confronted with Christ. We are not speaking of people in a Third World country, nor are we speaking about people who are part of a cult. These are people in your neighborhood right now who believe they have

It is people, of course, who advance wrong thinking and behavior. But to be effective in making it right in our communities, we must attack immoral principles, not people. It is not you they reject; it is the Truth, Jesus Himself. It is possible to "make it right" in our homes and in our churches. We can even begin making it right in our communities. "If the foundations be destroyed, what can the righteous do?" (Ps. 11:3 KJV). We can recover "the fear of God" in ourselves and in our families and churches, acknowledging Him as the Source of all good things.[4]

—Josh D. McDowell,
author and speaker

31

never been confronted with the reality of their sin and challenged to respond to Jesus Christ. It is not that these people have never heard of Christ, and many of these individuals have even been to some type of religious ceremony or service. Yet they are convinced that no one has taken the time to carefully and clearly share the gospel with them.

Due to the craziness of life, many of us are rushing from one obligation to another, and I am the first to stand guilty. In fact, one study conducted on senior pastors found that one of the major reasons pastors do not share their faith is the obligations they have to the church. Most young ministers have a fire in their bones (see Jer. 20:9) to share God's Word with anyone with whom they come in contact. But over time, church obligations and duties prevent ministers from going into the community and being used to change lives. A youth minister responded to our inquiry with the following: "The passion I have had to share my faith has been doused with the routines of church life. The only way to fuel the flames is to challenge myself to be involved with training my students to share their faith and then to lead by example." This young man had an insight into one of the trends that has been discovered: we are to be intentional in our evangelism if we are going to see lives changed in our communities.

What is the mission of the church? Why do we exist? We exist to be involved in fulfilling the Great Commission. Do you remember the commercial that showed two completely different companies trying to coexist? A beauty salon doubles as a chain saw repair shop; a mechanic's business also is a law firm; or my favorite, the fast-food burger joint that doubles as a pest control company! Do you see the disconnection? So it is with the church when we are involved in anything and everything—except the one calling we have upon our lives. Evangelism must be the central, primary focus of the church.

2

Own Up

Integrity Is an Attention-Grabber

In times like these men should utter nothing for which they would not be willingly responsible through time and in eternity.

—Abraham Lincoln

My remedy for insomnia is to watch as many infomercials as possible. But some of the thirty-minute presentations really do convince you that their product will change your life. One particular info-sales-guru came across with so much sincerity that I was about to call and order the "chance of a lifetime" product.

In an ironic turn of events, I switched channels and found a rough and tough professional wrestling match. The guys were brawny and the girls as tough as they come. As I watched the match, I noticed how many people in the stands were engaged

Christ is the epitome of integrity, which the Merriam-Webster dictionary defines as "firm adherence to a code of especially moral or artistic values," or "incorruptibility." The incorruptibility of Jesus is evident in the way he handled every harsh word, every flesh-tearing snap of the whip, every encounter with demons, and every temptation Satan threw at him. Jesus modeled integrity at every turn, and we, as Christians, are called to do the same. Psalm 15:2–5 says, "He who walks with integrity, and works righteousness, and speaks truth in his heart. He does not slander with his tongue, nor does evil to his neighbor, nor takes up a reproach against his friend; in whose eyes a reprobate is despised, but who honors those who fear the LORD; he swears to his own hurt and does not change; he does not put out his money at interest, nor does he take a bribe against the innocent. He who does these things will never be shaken."

—David Edwards, evangelist and author

in the canvas carousel that was taking place. I do not know if the fans knew it was fake or not, but they were all outraged at the villain who plainly broke all of the rules and was disqualified from the match.

Finally, I turned the channel again and found religious programming. Now I believe in getting the message of Jesus to everyone by every means possible, but this particular program caused me to take a step back. It was just as energetic as the infomercial and just as engaging as the wrestling. Could the world be looking at the message of Jesus Christ in the same way they see infomercials or other entertainment? Even worse, have our communities now placed the church in the same arena as wrestling—leaving the picture of the church to the few radicals, a picture that the masses, like the wrestling fans, have not realized is fake?

With the plurality of religious choices in our country today, there is a call for believers to live what they say they believe. Clear and simple, we must be authentic in our faith and live with integrity.

According to the Princeton Dictionary, *authentic* means "conforming to fact and therefore worthy of belief; a reliable account by an eyewitness." Our witness must be authentic, which means our actions have to reflect the power of our words. Have you ever been up late at night watching one of those old international films that was obviously dubbed into English? If so, you have no doubt encountered the arduous task of trying to match the audio with the video. The lips are moving, but you hear nothing—then you hear words without lips moving. These experiences prove troubling for movie lovers who want to follow the plot. The same problem exists when we are called to share our faith. The world expects a follower of Jesus Christ to have the audio match the video. Paul says, "But God's strong foundation continues to stand. These words are written on the seal: 'The Lord knows those who belong to him,' and 'Everyone who wants to belong to the Lord must stop doing wrong'" (2 Tim. 2:19 NCV).

A pastor we surveyed wrote, "Evangelism will be based not on what we are doing, but who we are. The world is watching. Ministry foundations will be laid by character and integrity." Most studies will convince us that organized religion has fallen down on most people's priority lists, but the sensitivity to wanting a personal relationship with God is on the increase. It is imperative that the body of Christ shine brightly in a dark world.

Phil Cooke, a consultant to some of the leading nonprofit organizations in America, writes in his blog,

> Whenever I work with non-profit or religious leaders in trying to brand their organizations, I usually ask the man or woman at the top, "What makes you different?" In other words, "What personal trait separates you from the pack?" The first response I invariably get is "authenticity." I get that answer over and over. Many pastors and ministry leaders are especially proud of their authenticity, and feel like they are one of the few who have it. But that usually leaves me a bit depressed. Not because

this person really is authentic, but because they consider it so special and rare. After all, shouldn't "authenticity" be normal for pastors and ministry leaders? Shouldn't authenticity be the baseline behavior for any spiritual or non-profit leader? Isn't it a bit sad that we live in an era where "authenticity" is considered a rare trait for pastors and ministry leaders?

But then again, after seeing the divorces, lawsuits, legal actions, and financial questions non-profit and ministry leaders have been facing over the last number of months, perhaps being authentic is more rare than we'd like to think.[1]

We must find out how we can overcome the lack of authenticity of our witness. This leads to another important question, "How can inauthentic witnesses creep into the church?" Acts 8 gives us an example of someone who was not authentic in the faith. His name is Simon, and he is amazed at what he sees Philip the evangelist doing in Samaria. Verses 9–13 tell of his conversion and baptism. When Peter and John come on the scene, he becomes more intrigued to the point that he is willing to pay money for the use of the spiritual power of "giving" the Holy Spirit to believers. An important spiritual truth can be applied from this passage. Many times in the church a new believer's excitement can be mishandled. It is true that a new believer can be a strong witness for Christ, but he or she is not necessarily an immediate spiritual leader. There is something called *instant success* but nothing called *instant maturity*. The problem is not the desire to be used spiritually but the process of being used. It is impossible to explain something you yourself do not understand.

In answer to Simon's request to buy the power of giving the Holy Spirit, the apostles give him a stern warning: "You and your money should both be destroyed, because you thought you could buy God's gift with money" (Acts 8:20 NCV).

Simon's false conversion shows us several principles that lead to an inauthentic witness. First, he is fixated on the results, not the true Power Source. The term *amazed* is used four times in this chapter in connection with Simon. He is convinced that amazement leads to success. The power Philip possesses is meant to change lives, not to turn heads. Second, Simon's desires are not surrendered before the Lord. Remember, it is after Simon is baptized and has been around Philip that the apostles give him the stern warning. Sometimes a believer will ask the Lord for his blessings, power, and mercy without first surrendering before his lordship. Finally, Simon tries to gain God's power by man's mechanisms. He has the money and thinks that is what makes the world turn. But God's power is given not to those with the most wealth, education, or opportunities but to those he desires. Simon's wrong approach is duplicated with the same results countless times in our nation today.

Paul warns believers to not defraud one another (1 Thess. 4:6). To me, another definition of *defraud* is "falsely advertise." This is the issue with someone like Simon in Acts. Over and over I have seen immature believers try to take a position of influence by saying things they do not believe or acting in ways they normally do not act. Authenticity is not a switch you turn on and off at a whim but rather a sure foundation for your life in every circumstance. Anything but authenticity should be considered the exception to the rule. It should be our muscle and not our pulse—a pulse goes up and down based on feelings, situations, or circumstances; a muscle stays consistent through every situation. Authenticity should be the muscle we flex in our everyday life and not the pulse that races out of control.

A Trustworthy Witness

The world is not searching for another carnival coming to town. As one pastor shared, "The lost world is not looking for another fancy presentation. They are looking for hope and a genuine individual sharing the simple message of the Gospel." I do not know how to communicate "how to be authentic in three simple steps" and sound, well, authentic. Authenticity must be centrally located in your life to be genuine. We may not know exactly how to be authentic, but we can definitely tell when we are not.

Remember the infomercial salesman I discussed in the introduction of this chapter? He came across as sincere and truthful that his product was life changing: a three-carat diamond ring for $19.95. To some it seemed too good to be true. I imagine customers receiving their ring and opening it with excitement. When the box is opened, however, the reality sets in—the truth is you can't buy a genuine diamond ring for twenty bucks. Remember, the definition of authenticity is giving a reliable account. It is more than being sincere; it is being trustworthy.

Responses of People Who Live by Character
(from Psalm 15:2–5 NASB)

1. They do right—work righteousness (v. 2).
2. They deal with their mistakes—walk with integrity (v. 2).
3. They delight in honesty—speak truth in their hearts (v. 2).
4. They discipline their words—do not slander with their tongues (v. 3).
5. They defend the righteous—honor those who fear the Lord (v. 4).
6. They deliver the goods—swear to their own hurt and do not change (v. 4).
7. They distribute their wealth—do not put out their money at interest (v. 5).
8. They do not use others—do not take a bribe against the innocent (v. 5).[2]

—David Edwards, evangelist and author

As important as authenticity is in the witness of believers, integrity must also fill their life. Pat Williams describes integrity like this: "The origin of the word makes its meaning very clear. 'Integrity' comes from the Latin adjective *integer*, which means 'whole' or 'complete.' In mathematics, an integer is a positive or negative whole number or zero—number without any fractional part." He continues. "A person of integrity is honest and upright. His soul is not divided or compartmentalized."[3] Over the next few years there will be an increasing amount of scrutiny on the witness of believers in Jesus Christ, and now as always, integrity should be the standard for our lives. An October 2007 *USA Today* article stated,

> A generation ago, people turned to trusted authorities such as newspapers and mainline churches to get information. But trust in such institutions has fallen over the past 30 years, eroding the relationship between Americans and a number of traditional sources of trust. A poll called the General Social Survey has asked people whether they have "a great deal of confidence" in social institutions, and their answers reveal a clear decline.
>
> According to this survey by the National Opinion Research Center at the University of Chicago, confidence has dropped since the 1970s in . . . organized religion [from] 35% to 24%.[4]

We see this by the downplaying of spiritual issues by society. Businesspeople now look in disdain at business cards that have any Christian symbol. One businessman said, "When I see a business card with a Christian symbol, I immediately put my hand on my wallet because I know I am about to be robbed."

American Culture Craves Integrity

As many in society view Christians with scorn, our integrity must not waiver. Jesus tells us we are the light of the world

(Matt. 5:14–16), and the light always shines the brightest at the darkest moments. Our communities are facing some very dark moments. Integrity in evangelism is extremely important for several reasons:

1. Nothing is secure.
2. Everything is subjective.
3. In our society, anything goes.
4. Something must connect.

First, *nothing is secure.* From the fluctuating economy to threats of terrorism, from worries about our children's safety and future to our own private grief and broken dreams, Americans' sense of security is shaky at best. Identity theft is rampant in our society; everyone feels like their security is in jeopardy. Friendships are now born out of skepticism and deceit rather than in bettering one another's life. Due to this insecurity, individuals are in need of friendships that can be trusted. More than ever, a good name is more valuable than silver and gold (Prov. 22:1). Integrity is an attractive trait for people in our culture who do not trust easily or often.

Second, *everything is subjective.* In our society of virtual reality, there is a plethora of information that causes doubt in every absolute, whether based on facts or folklore. The Internet makes every issue open to debate and every value questioned. For every website that promotes Christianity, there is another that ridicules it. Although many may debate our beliefs and the Bible, we must live our lives so they cannot debate our integrity.

Third, *anything goes* in our society. Teachers, preachers, politicians, and people from every other profession have been paraded across our televisions with immoral stories that seem unbelievable to mainstream America. Scandals of cheating run rampant through every facet of professional sports. One columnist exclaimed that now little children can "pick their sports heroes by their method of cheating not by their play." If everyone cheats, who can really tell the right score? For a believer in today's society, there is unparalleled temptation to be like everyone else. We must refrain from the tendency and go one more step: remove the temptation. We are to treat sin as the enemy, not as a friend. Yes, love the sinner, but leave a person's presence when he or she sins. Integrity is compromised when we say someone needs Jesus but approve of that person's actions by association.

Fourth, *something must connect.* In my opinion Starbucks has hit a gold mine—not in coffee but in community. Walk into any Starbucks and you will see throngs of college students or retirees who have staked out their little corner for social networking. The company almost begs their customers to sit and enjoy the *experience* of Starbucks. People are no longer searching for events to attend but, like Starbucks, experiences to connect with their peers. With everything so shallow in our society, individuals are searching for a place to buy in and plant roots in their lives.

Hypocrites or Jesus's Followers?

The church has an incredible opportunity for people to buy into community. There is a church in our city that has a Family Life Center (gym) that is never open. While attending a lunch for a city event, I asked the pastor why they did not utilize such a center for community outreach. Think of the kids, families, even seniors who would love to come to events in this type of facility. His answer was saddening. He said that the church did utilize it when they first built it, but some unchurched teenagers started hanging out there. This scared the church members to the point that the church authorities finally decided that if it was going to attract people like that, they would just close it down. The church must understand that our society views it as an exclusive joint of hypocrites, not a united, caring, loving group of Jesus's followers. We must open the doors to allow people to join our community.

The church also needs to pay attention to the scenarios playing out in our neighborhoods. Most homes are not made up of two parents, two children, a picket fence, and a dog. There are now single parents with two jobs and latchkey children searching for deep meaning in their lives. Look around for the places in your community where you can tap into one of the concerns in your community. Become a volunteer at a local elementary school, start a small, weekly Bible study at a coffee house, or provide a networking meeting for single parents where they can receive emotional, spiritual, and social support.

A great illustration of this is a friend of mine who developed a men's Bible study in his home. It started out as a small gathering of friends twenty years ago, and it still meets every Saturday morning with forty men. He speaks of men who have gone through the suffering and pain of losing jobs, terminal illness, or divorce. It is more than a Bible study—it is a community. Most of the attendees have come to know Christ as a result of this study. It is a sight to see his living room filled to capacity every Saturday morning. After the study and prayer, the men fill the kitchen, porch, and every other area to eat a full breakfast cooked for them by the leader's wife. It takes a serious commitment to see someone come to know Christ.

Integrity has been uncovered as the main ingredient for effective evangelism over the next ten years according to the thousands of people I have polled. As one leading denominational leader responded, "Evangelism will be very much in the context of a secular society. . . . They must believe in us as we share about believing in him." In communication classes we learn that it is my responsibility, as the deliverer, to communicate my message to you clearly, not your responsibility to receive what I am saying. We should never presume our friends know that we have integrity; we should live our lives as an example of integrity. Therefore, what are some differences between evangelism with integrity and evangelism without integrity?

People with integrity are more concerned with the eternal perspective, not the temporal. In the early church, the notion of planning for retirement was foreign. In reality, we are not supposed to be comfortable with all the materialistic items offered to us. I remember having a meeting in Oklahoma City for a group of people. The hotel management found out that the former mayor (who was in office when the hotel was built) and a famous businessman from the city were scheduled to speak at the meeting, during which we had arranged to have a dessert served. When we walked into the room for the dessert function, I was expecting the usual cookie and coffee spread. Was I wrong! The entire room was filled with every possible after-dinner delicacy. This was all done for a total of twenty-seven people. Every time we took a dessert, the item was replaced with an exact duplicate. We had not ordered this dessert, and I profusely apologized throughout the evening. It was embarrassing thinking so much waste was happening under my guard. In addition, the conference was about making an impact on the community, and there we were subjecting ourselves to the extreme of chocolate pleasure. At the end of the evening we packed up seven boxes of dessert to send out for the businessman's employees to enjoy the next day.

This experience reminded me to be sensitive to live for the essentials and leave the rest behind. Most of us treat our temporary residence as if it is the eternal resting place. Just as you would not check into a hotel for one night and upon entering your room start redecorating it, we should not be so consumed with building this life. People around us know how seriously we take our convictions by where we place our resources.

Arrogant Ministry

Integrity is also about serving others rather than striving for our personal gain. Jesus came among us to serve, and we are to imitate his example. Rick Warren has remarked that one of the strongest issues facing us in reaching our communities is the arrogance that is enshrined in ministry. Most of us are eager to share our latest numbers and quick to spin any statistic that is not favorable about our ministry. Throughout Scripture, however, there are strict warnings about pride. For instance, 1 Peter 5:5 says, "God resists the proud but gives grace to the humble" (NKJV). Some people interpret the word *resist* as *stiff-arm*. I'd rather go up against the largest professional football offensive lineman than have God Almighty stiff-arm me. So many times, however, I find myself struggling, only to lose the fight for myself. Jesus tells us that "whoever finds his life will lose it, and whoever loses his life for my sake will find it" (Matt. 10:39). Ironically, Jesus reminds us that if we are so consumed with ourselves, our life will slip through our fingers, but if we lose ourselves to serve others, our lives can develop true significance.

Integrity is also about *significance*, not *success*. Success is defined with extreme subjectivity and without many measurable benchmarks. Significance should be measured by numbers—numbers not for numbers' sake but for eternity's sake, with each number representing a person's soul. I was always discouraged about keeping a record of numbers in ministry. From the beginning, the ministry I serve has been careful to keep accurate records of those making decisions. I did not really know why at first, but I knew it must be done. It was not until I studied John 21:1–14 that I discovered a great reason. When Jesus told the disciples where to cast their nets, the fish filled the nets over the brim. When the disciples got the fish to the shore, they counted each fish and came up with an exact total of 153. It was not about numbers for numbers' sake, but each number represented one that had been caught. A life of significance is not about increasing numbers for numbers' sake, but each one that comes to Christ represents another one in the net to present to Christ. If there is one or 153, each one is a life that has been impacted with the gospel.

Integrity is also about staying consistent even during crises. When I first met Billy Graham, I was with several other young evangelists. When we saw him approaching, one of the evangelists ran up to him and began to shake his hand repeatedly saying, "Dr. Graham, I want you to know that I have modeled my ministry after yours since the beginning!" At first I thought I should have run faster than my friend, and honestly, the lesson that followed was eye-opening. Dr. Graham stepped back and began to blush. He started shaking his head and said, "No, don't model yourself after me. I have made too many mistakes. Model your ministry after Christ." My friend did not intend to put Dr. Graham in the role of an idol, but even here Dr. Graham had trained himself to deflect any attention given to him back to Christ. After Dr. Graham left our group, one young guy said, "He really does not know who he is." May we all strive to attain this level of integrity in our lives.

A final thought about integrity is another insight from Pat Williams, my dear friend with the Orlando Magic in Orlando, Florida. He says,

> One synonym for integrity is sincerity—the state of being truthful, genuine, and free of deception or duplicity. The word "sin-

45

cerity" comes from the Latin word, *sincerus*, meaning "clean and pure through and through." The Latin word, *sincerus*, comes from two Latin root words, *sine* ("without") and *cera* ("wax"). Tradition tells us that dishonest Roman sculptors would cover up nicks and flaws in their statues with a wax filler. The deception would last only until a hot summer sun melted the wax and exposed the flaws. A sculpture that was pure and flawless was said to be *sine cera*, "without wax."[5]

As we embark on the journey of reaching our communities for Christ, we need to be sure that we have a solid foundation that allows the hearer to believe in us as we introduce to them the one they are searching to find.

Can We Regain Our Integrity?

Finally, take note of how to begin again. I have a dear friend, Dr. John Corts, former president and COO of the Billy Graham Evangelistic Association, who has a fireproof remedy to overcome a lack of integrity and stop the revolving door of good intention followed by failure. It is the biblical concept of confession. When the Holy Spirit reveals in your life an area of pretense, an act that communicates differently than the true intent, acknowledge it to yourself as *sin* (with the repulsion and horror of that which required the cross of Jesus). Then confess it immediately to the Lord and agree with God about what occurred and the judgment on it.

In our modern culture, however, we seem more intent on *saving face* with others than being right with God. So one step more may stir a change in us: go back in repentance and confess the pretense or the untruth with the person or persons who witnessed your deceit, your lie, or your playacting. Be forthright in seeking their help to hold you accountable. Your friends, family, employees, and fellow believers already know about the integrity gap, but you need to confront it to the point of saying it aloud. When you fail again, confess again fully to yourself, to God, and to those who were affected. That's true repentance, and the sorrow and shame of correcting the wrong becomes a goad to stir change in yourself to be an authentic person of integrity.

Of course in instances that involve legal, marital, or personal impropriety, please consult with godly counsel to find biblical means to handling the correction. It will not take long to discover the joyous freedom that comes when you stay purposefully in a state of integrity with your conscience clear of worry that someone might discover the whole truth about you. Granted, integrity by itself will not win this world to Christ, but without it the entire community will be placing faith in the same category with infomercials and wrestling matches, while wondering if Jesus's message is true or false.

3

LISTEN UP

Connect by Listening

More people have been brought into the church by the kindness of real Christian love than by all the theological arguments in the world, and more people have been driven from the church by the hardness and ugliness of so-called Christians than by all the doubts in the world.

—William Barclay, Scottish theologian and writer

Several years ago, my good friend Luis Palau wrote an evangelistic book that generated numerous responses from readers. One stands out among the rest—it was from a gentleman named Ryan, a lecturer at a major university in England.

After getting drunk on New Year's Eve 2000, Ryan woke up with a hangover that wouldn't quit. He felt disgusted by his decadent behavior the previous night. Desperate to turn over a new leaf, Ryan went to a local bookshop looking for answers. There he found the British edition of Palau's book. Afterward, Ryan started corresponding with David, one of Palau's associates:

> I would very much appreciate your advice. I am a twenty-four-year-old teacher with a great interest in philosophy and religion. I have lived an agnostic life, dearly wishing to find something to truly believe but never quite getting there, being thrown off by confusions and disillusionment. I have recently started reading the Bible and your book. . . .
>
> Despite a life of trusting science and whatever I could see, hear, and touch for myself, I am more than willing to accept that there are many things way beyond my comprehension, and I would love to become a true Christian. But I have found difficulty in accepting Christ as real and, although I know it is the wrong thing to ask, I wish I could have some proof or conviction in my heart upon which to base my faith. I pray many times daily, asking for God's guidance in finding the right path to tread, and here I am.
>
> I will continue to read the Bible, but can you advise me on what else I can do to find faith? . . .
>
> At the moment I have many questions about all that I have read, including many sections of the Bible that either don't make sense to me or seem to contradict each other. However, in my years of searching for truth, my reason and logic have failed me, so I am willing to put these aside for a while. How can I find faith? I can conceive of the ideas of God, Christ, the crucifixion and resurrection, but they don't feel real to me. I'm not giving up yet.

Sadly, it's not always safe to express such honest, searching words in church. If one doesn't get rebuffed, he or she is often lectured. What today's seekers need is someone who will really *listen* to their stories—not just point out where they went wrong.

Successful evangelism strategies today need to focus on the person and his or her need for Jesus Christ. How can we do that?

1. *Listen, don't lecture.* In David's reply, he told Ryan: "Please let me make it clear I'd prefer to be a facilitator—not an 'answer man'—when it comes to exploring your questions. After all, it doesn't really matter what I think or believe. So please don't take anything I say as gospel truth."

> I want spiritual seekers to find a safe place to get answers that will satisfy their hearts and minds. The doors of our ministries are wide open to people who want to scrutinize the faith and see if it makes sense. So often I see that as their questions are answered and their concerns are addressed, they end up becoming followers of Jesus.
>
> —Bill Hybels, Willow Creek Community Church

Ryan explained that he had been christened as a child but almost never went to church as a teenager or young adult. By this point he was visiting a prominent denominational church, but he still felt disillusioned when the minister indicated he believed "that although passages in the Bible can help us toward an understanding of God, they are not necessarily true." That didn't make sense to Ryan.

2. *Walk through trials together.* A few days later Ryan wrote:

> I have been through a fairly bad few days recently. I have yet to find faith, although I have prayed many times each day. I have been getting worse since I last wrote to you. I desperately want to have faith, but my lack of success so far and my uncertainties have all piled upon me and I have felt thoroughly wretched for some time. My sleeping pattern is in ruin, and I have eaten very little in the last few days, having hardly any appetite.
>
> I have tried telling Jesus that I am ready for him to come into my life, but I don't know how. I just feel like a wretched sinner calling out into emptiness.

A few days ago I stopped off at a different church in the city center and spoke briefly with a minister there. We prayed together, which I felt good about, but I have felt extremely lonely ever since.

You say it seems as if I'm very close to becoming a Christian. I hope that's true. I really want to let Jesus Christ into my life and know that my sins are forgiven and that there is a great meaning to my life after all. Confessing my sins has just made me feel worse lately. Every time I confess and apologize to God for losing my temper in class, using bad language among friends, etc., I just feel worse.

Perhaps my current melancholy is related to a current change of lifestyle—since I made a vow to myself to "find" God, I have not been out drinking, have stopped spending a long time on computer games, have stopped buying useless artifacts on whimsical shopping trips, etc. Perhaps dropping these habits is taking some getting used to. It was my twenty-fifth birthday last Sunday, and I didn't enjoy it.

I'm not giving up yet, but I am finding everything very hard going. I find myself looking back nostalgically to when life was "enjoyable."

What should I do now?

What would you have told Ryan?

3. *Emphasize hope in Christ.* At this point Ryan was in despair, and David feared he might become suicidal. So David gave Ryan his home email address and kept corresponding with him that weekend, emphasizing the sure hope we can have in Jesus Christ.

On Saturday evening, Ryan told David:

I made a kind of vow to myself last night that I was tired of beating about bushes that were getting me nowhere. I vowed that this weekend I would do whatever I could to cover some ground.

I just prayed a few minutes ago. I told God that although I don't understand how electricity works, I still trust a light to come on when I press a switch. Although I don't know how an engine works, I still trust cars and buses to carry me. Even though I don't understand God, Jesus, the Holy Spirit, the Bible . . . I am willing to trust in them. I told God that I have little faith, but with what little faith I have I asked Jesus to come into my life and I would go wherever he leads me. I desperately thanked God for his gifts and prayed dearly for my tiny spark of faith to grow. I told God I would consider myself to be a Christian from this point on, although currently a weak one.

I hope my words today have not been empty. I don't feel different (although I wasn't expecting rays of light and flashes of lightning). I hope I can grow a little more in faith before doubts settle in.

All I can do at the moment, I think, is to spend today getting my strength and resolve back. Tomorrow I will go to church and try to trust all of the words I hear there. And I'll continue to pray for the gift of faith. Thanks again.

Taking advantage of the time zone difference between England and the western United States, David wrote back to Ryan that same evening. He affirmed his commitment to trust Jesus Christ and become a Christian—what a life-changing night that proved to be! Yet sadly, David also had to urge Ryan *not* to trust all the words he heard at church, especially given the unbelief of that particular church's pastor.

4. *Point toward a good church.* At that point Ryan was attending three different churches—checking them all out, as it were. David encouraged him to join one that (1) wholeheartedly worships the Lord, (2) believes the Bible, (3) proclaims salvation in Jesus Christ, and (4) welcomes new members.

Based on that criteria, Ryan selected a church to call home—but not before he asked David to choose for him. David turned it around and said he needed to make that decision for himself.

He also encouraged Ryan to keep reading God's Word and praying.

A little later that same evening, David received another email from Ryan. It clearly showed that God was already at work in his life.

> I thought I'd check my email before bed and was pleased once more to hear from you. Having read Matthew and Mark, I wanted to take a peek ahead, as in school I never studied any of the books that follow the Gospels.
>
> I started reading Acts (the first seven chapters)—I found this to be brilliant reading, and it left me feeling good. It gives such a strong and positive message! The sheer narrative momentum captured me. It shows just how powerful and unstoppable true faith really is. Even the persecutions and stoning of the apostles bring courage to mind rather than grief.

Thankfully, those opening chapters of Acts gave Ryan a new understanding of what the church is all about.

Ryan concluded that evening's letter by saying, "Thank you once again for staying in communication with me—I'm sure I would have been lost without your help these last few weeks. I can't seem to shake the expectation that going to church tomorrow will be good for me."

Thankfully, the church he chose to attend *was* good—that Sunday, that Wednesday, and each week thereafter. While the two men continued to correspond, Ryan applied to become a member of that local church and soon was flourishing under its nurturing care. What a joy to see someone's life turn around so dramatically!

As evangelists, we have been commissioned to share a message of hope—not a menu of rules and regulations. That means welcoming those, like Ryan, who may be agnostics, doubters, or other spiritual seekers. By meeting them on their turf, we can build a relationship of acceptance and trust that will draw them toward the person of Jesus Christ.

What We're Up Against

In John 10:10 Jesus gives us the devil's game plan: "The thief comes only to steal and kill and destroy; I have come that they may have life, and have it to the full." Satan's tactic is to "steal"—to *lure away*. According to the American Cancer Society, 95 percent of all people who smoke marijuana started off on some form of tobacco. One step leads to another step. No one wakes up one morning and says, "I want to destroy my life." It is always a regression as a person is slowly lured away from what is right until he or she is tumbling down a path toward destruction.

The word *kill* means to "draw the breath out from." Interestingly, the word *breath* in the Bible often refers to the Holy Spirit. I don't want to get into a discussion about whether you can lose your salvation, but the principle here is this: it's not the presence of God in your life but the passion for God inside your life that dies. Once the devil has successfully lured someone away, slowly but surely that passion for God is drained from his or her life.

The word *destroy* means "to remove from existence." If you had a dry erase board and you wrote all the letters and numbers

Evangelism will be based not on what we are doing but on who we are. The world is watching. Ministry foundations will be laid by character and integrity. Recent surveys show Christianity the religion is "out" . . . but the person of Jesus is "in." We must get rid of all stumbling blocks, except the cross, to someone coming to have a personal relationship with Christ. We must be cautious not to lose spiritual authority for the sake of relevancy. Going to natural gathering places and events will provide good opportunities for evangelism.

—Rick Marshall, leadership consultant; former Billy Graham crusade and follow-up director on that board and then erased them, they would be gone. They could never be brought back. You could try to duplicate them by writing them on the board again, but the originals are gone. That's what Satan wants to do in every life.

Jesus is saying, "That's not my goal. I have come that you may have life abundantly, to the full—life on top of life." That is the greatest message we will ever hear! And it's a message that this generation desperately needs; it's never been more important that we know how to communicate to them and point them toward Jesus.

It's about Being Relevant

In 2003, born-again actor Stephen Baldwin got together with evangelist Kevin Palau to produce a forty-five-minute DVD called *Livin It*. The film featured top skateboarders and BMX riders doing tricks as well as sharing their testimonies about how they came to faith in Jesus Christ.

Evangelism is headed outside of the walls of the church. If a church is only content to reach those who feel safe enough to come inside their walls, that church could very well die.

You can take a course practically every week to learn a different way to share the gospel. The lost world is not looking for another fancy presentation—it is looking for hope and a genuine individual sharing the simple message.

—Johnson Ellis, CURA
Emergency Services

They hoped to sell at least 10,000 copies. Within eighteen months they had sold 100,000 copies of the DVD, and a sequel, *Livin It LA*, was rolled out on a red carpet in Los Angeles in 2006. Today the athletes are touring the country, putting on demos and outreach events, and sharing their message with crowds of excited young people.

Why the huge success? Is it because they have a big-name actor for a director? Or is it because the athletes can do some really awesome tricks? They probably both play a part in its success, but the thing that draws so many teenagers to the film is that it's *relevant*. They aren't being preached at or given a long list of rules or told they have to completely change their lifestyles. The *Livin It* films connect with them through a shared interest— skateboarding or BMX—and the guys simply share their stories. The Good News is communicated in a way that a new generation can understand, relate to, and appreciate.

An action sports DVD won't reach everyone, but it does speak to the thousands of teens and young adults who idolize skateboarders. The need is clear—whether it's our emergent generation or the baby boomers—we need to utilize the tools that will effectively reach people right where they are.

It's about Authenticity

Kids, teenagers, and even adults won't stick around long if they think they're going to be "preached at." People will often react somewhat negatively to being invited to a Sunday morning church service. But if you are putting on a concert, picnic, retreat, or festival, even unbelievers will be drawn to it. If you get involved in what they like doing, you then have a platform through which to introduce your message.

Not only is our generation looking for something relevant, they are also looking for something *authentic*. We live in a culture that has it all. Where else but the United States of America can you find a fast-food restaurant right next to a fast-weight-loss clinic? With so much stuff available to us, it is easy to get lost in it.

My nine-year-old son, Hunter, is an avid baseball fan. He loves to watch it, he loves to play it, and he loves to talk about it—he just lives for sports. One time he came to me and said, "Daddy, I want to be president of the United States!"

Beaming like a proud dad, I asked, "Why?"

"Because you get to throw the first pitch out at the World Series!" There's honesty for you!

It's okay to be real. Our Savior is a *real* person who cares for the needs of every individual. If you can relate to something an unbeliever is struggling with, share your story. Then explain how a relationship with God helped you get through. As Josh McDowell says, "Youth today process everything through their feelings and relationships. If you don't listen, they won't see the Gospel is relationally relevant."[1]

We don't want our children and our students to think that we preach *about* God; they need to realize that we *know* God. They have to understand it's all real in our lives. Start off with a smile. Isn't it great when you see a smile you're attracted to? Don't you hate it when you're around someone who doesn't have a smile? You immediately want to dart the other direction. Even if everything else is going wrong, and you can't find anything to smile about or get excited about, here's some good news—the tomb is empty, the throne is occupied, and Jesus Christ is Lord over all creation. I don't know about you, but that brings a smile to my face!

When we ask people why they don't share their faith, one of the top reasons is *fear*—fear of failure, fear of rejection. But we need to think beyond that. True, we might be rejected, but we might

> We have to understand our own faith and worldview well enough that we can accurately interpret what others are saying to us and respond to them with intelligent questions and answers. We should respectfully and lovingly ask them about their views, without trying to force our views upon others. Rather than criticize them for the errors of their thinking, it is far better to help them independently conclude that they are off base and need to reconsider their position. In America today, this is best accomplished through questions. No matter how inane someone's point of view may be, you cannot argue a person into the kingdom of God.
>
> —George Barna, Barna Research Group

also plant a seed that will lead to salvation. And even if we are rejected, 1 Peter 4:14 says, "If you are insulted because of the name of Christ, you are blessed, for the Spirit of glory and of God rests on you." There's no negative outcome. If we get to lead a new believer into God's kingdom, what a thrill! But even if we're rejected, we're blessed. The next time someone slams a door in your face, just stand up and say, "Praise the Lord!"

Reaching the Heart of Our Generation

When I was in school, I wasn't the greatest math student. Between fractions, algebra, geometry, and calculus, I was barely keeping my head above water. But I've really come to love one particular type of math—multiplication, specifically spiritual multiplication. For example, one person shares Jesus Christ with ten people. Then each of those ten people shares with another ten people. Now that group of people shares with another ten people each. Suddenly you've got hundreds and hundreds of people receiving Jesus Christ. Now that's some awesome spiritual multiplication happening! And it's all because one person stepped out and told others about Jesus Christ.

Years ago Ezra Kimball, a Sunday school teacher in Boston, felt burdened to share the gospel with a member of his class who worked as a shoe clerk. So one day he nervously cornered the boy and stumbled through the gospel message. He left feeling discouraged about his weak attempt at witnessing, but later that day D. L. Moody trusted Jesus Christ as his Savior because Ezra had obeyed the Lord. Then:

> Moody became the foremost American evangelist of the nineteenth century. God used him to awaken a heart for evangelism in Fredrick D. Meyer, pastor of a small British church.

Meyer later came to America on a speaking tour, and during a speech on a college campus, J. Wilbur Chapman came to Christ.

Chapman followed in the steps of Moody and employed former baseball player turned YMCA clerk Billy Sunday to help him with evangelism.

Billy Sunday held a revival in Charlotte, North Carolina. A group of men at the revival were so excited that they planned another outreach, bringing evangelist Mordecai Hamm to town to preach.

One evening when Hamm gave the invitation, a boy by the name of Billy Graham went forward and trusted Christ.

I think we know the rest of the story.

All it takes is one person—stepping out, taking a chance, being real—to reach the hearts of this generation. It's a privilege to share the hope, joy, and peace found in Jesus. Ask God every day to give you a heart for the lost, because when you love people and see them as God does, you just *have* to tell them about him!

The time is ripe for our generation to have a new encounter with Jesus Christ. Let's pray that God will give us the tools and resources to connect with them and show them the blessings of eternal life.

4

Check Up

What Your Motives Reveal

Great opportunities to help others seldom come, but small ones surround us constantly.

—Unknown

Sitting down across from a homeless man named James to eat a Thanksgiving lunch at a mission was a learning experience. It immediately became clear that the usual small talk designed to meet and shape an opinion about a new acquaintance was unhelpful. *Where did you go to school? Tell me about your family. Where do you live? What do you do?* The inability to use even the smallest thing like "starter questions" makes it easy to see that poverty is a great divider. Deep misunderstandings easily grow between those who have resources and those who do not. Rather than placing ourselves in these types of uncomfortable situations, it can be simpler to avoid those who are not in our geographical, social, and religious circles at all. But we are coming to see that walking away from service, especially service leading to evangelism, is no longer an option.

In the last twenty years, American Christians have witnessed a shocking ideological shift. A generation ago, young people dreamed of spending their summer months relaxing by the pool or going on vacation. The most committed students would go on a retreat to either the mountains or the beach. Today students yearn to be more involved in contributing to building homes for the needy instead of visiting their beach home and to feeding the hungry instead of working at a country club. We have shifted into service mode and are

---

One of the clearest trends in evangelism today is the increase in intentional community service as a valid avenue to sharing the faith. There are some clear advantages to this trend:

It is biblical. Jesus often met a person's immediate need in conjunction with speaking about his Father's kingdom. He healed the lame, touched the leper, fed the hungry, and more.

It is personal. People are often skeptical about discussing matters of faith with strangers. One practical demonstration of God's love can open the door to ongoing conversation. It also helps the Christian understand where the person is in relationship to Jesus and how to engage in conversation.

It is team-driven. Service evangelism is often done in groups and allows for pairing up experienced people with those new to outreach. This style recognizes a variety of gifts as necessary to communicate the message of the gospel.

It is exponential. Some Christians are too frightened to engage in gospel conversation. Demonstrating the faith helps include more people in evangelism and often encourages the timid to move from helping to verbalizing what they believe.

—José Zayas, international evangelist and author

---

realizing the value of getting our hands dirty while keeping our hearts pure.

Motives

What is the purpose of service? We assist those in need because Jesus commands us to do so. In Matthew 25:35–36 Jesus tells us to feed the hungry, invite the homeless into our home, give clothes to those without clothes, take care of the sick, and visit those in prison. In the Sermon on the Mount Jesus cautions us,

> Be careful not to do your "acts of righteousness" before men, to be seen by them. If you do, you will have no reward from your Father in heaven. So when you give to the needy, do not announce it with trumpets, as the hypocrites do in the synagogues and on the streets, to be honored by men. I tell you the truth, they have received their reward in full. But when you give to the needy, do not let your left hand know what your right hand is doing, so that your giving may be in secret. Then your Father, who sees what is done in secret, will reward you."
>
> Matthew 6:1–4

His point? Pure motives are extremely important. Our intentions must spring out of our passion to help others and share Christ, not to make ourselves look good to others or make us feel good about ourselves.

Regardless of your economic and social status, no matter how high or low, there are always comparisons made. Someone may look at the "other side of the fence" and see it as more attractive than what they have. At the same time, we may look the other direction and easily see those who are less fortunate: families unable to make ends meet from week to week; individuals without power, possessions, prestige, or popularity. We can see this segment of our society and feel guilty because of what we have. But our seeking to help others should not be driven by the desire to lessen any guilt we may have as a result of the blessings we have received. We should not help the person asking for handouts at the street corner just because we feel bad about sitting in our comfortable, air-conditioned cars; we should help them in order to improve their situation.

Hand in Hand

God has designed us with two hands that have the ability to work independently but are much more effective when working as a pair. Playing sports, strumming a musical instrument, turning the pages of a book, utilizing technology—two hands make each of these basic areas of our life more efficient. So it is with sharing Christ in today's society.

When reaching out to individuals in need, there are two hands that work best together. One hand is that of speaking a gospel presentation to someone, and the other hand is that of meeting someone's physical need. Ephesians 5:1–2 says, "Be imitators of God, therefore, as dearly loved children, and live a life of love, just as Christ loved us and gave himself up for us as a fragrant offering and sacrifice to God."

God loves us physically and spiritually. The first announcement of the birth of Jesus came to shepherds who were considered the working class of the day. Jesus was born in a stable and laid in an animal feeding trough. He was raised as a carpenter in a community overlooked by most. Even in his three years of earthly ministry, Jesus states that he, the Son of Man, has no home of his own—not even a place to lay his head (Luke 9:58). Jesus understands the poor because he too is poor. He becomes angry and overturns the tables of the money changers when he sees they are taking advantage of the poor in the shadow of the temple.

But even more important than taking care of the physically poor, Jesus is concerned about people who are poor spiritually. In Luke 9:10–17, Jesus feeds five thousand people with two fish and five loaves, but he does so in order to teach them about the kingdom of God and cure those who are ill (v. 11). In Luke 5:17–25, before Jesus heals the paralyzed man, he tells him "your sins are forgiven" (v. 20). We too must be equally concerned about people's physical and spiritual health.

When we reach out to people with two hands to address their physical and spiritual needs, we also need properly working hands, each with four fingers and a thumb. Try shaking hands with someone without using your thumb. It can be an awkward experience. So can attempting to be Christ's hands and feet if we try to do it ourselves, without Christ leading us.

In classic *Peanuts* style, Charlie Brown is watching television when Lucy approaches him and boldly requests the remote control. Charlie Brown asks her to give him one good reason why he should give her the remote. Lucy slowly counts her five fingers, making them into a fist that she holds in Charlie Brown's face and says, "Here are five good reasons." Charlie Brown immediately gives her the remote. As he walks out of the room looking at his five fingers, he asks himself why his fingers never get organized like that.

Five "organized fingers" of our ministry hand are: (1) recognizing a need, (2) being real or authentic, (3) respecting those who need help, (4) building relationships, and (5) taking responsibility. We start with the little finger of *recognizing a need* in a person's life. It has been said that to recognize a need is the same as recognizing a calling. It does not take long to look at today's culture and see many needs. There are people who are hurting financially, physically, emotionally, legally, relationally, and spiritually. Think of the challenges and adversities you have faced in your life. Were there times you faced job loss and financial uncertainties, torn relationships and difficult family situations, personal or family-related health crises or even death? These are the times we can allow the Lord to help us grow closer to him and become stronger as a result of life's adversities. Now what do you do with this new supernatural strength? Look for individuals who may be going through similar situations as yours and help them see how the Lord carried you through that time. Gently show by your own experience that he can carry them through too.

Does your heart ache for those who are hungry, homeless, in prisons, or in hospitals? This may be the Lord prompting you to get involved in helping individuals and families in need. Begin looking around to see how their needs are being met and learn how they are being helped by existing organizations and ministries. Ministries today need volunteers to help carry out their services. When you partner with active ministries, they can teach you how to better help those you know are hurting.

The ring finger holds the necessity to *be real or authentic* in your life and work to help others. Life defined by living from challenge to challenge gives people good instincts about others. For some people, correctly reading those with whom they come into contact is necessary for survival. People in need are smart and can tell if you are trying to make yourself feel better or look better to others. A volunteer prison ministry leader once told me inmates appreciate volunteers more than they appreciate the prison staff because volunteers do not have to visit. Repeated visits by a volunteer can open the door for relationships, and from those relationships come real evangelistic ministry opportunities.

Establishing credibility with people in need is essential to laying the foundation for ministering to them. Joe Aldrich from Multnomah Bible College challenges Christians: "People do not care what we know about Christ until they know we care about them as individuals." A person in need wants to be considered a person, not a project. Coming one time into someone's life with great fanfare of food, clothing, or gifts can be viewed as a gesture of kindness but rarely convinces that person to open up his or her life to the benefactor at the intimate level of spirituality. Through consistency of visits with an individual, you begin to have an authentic relationship that can ultimately allow you to share the gospel.

The middle finger of a helping hand is *respecting those who need help*. A ministry leader in a city preparing for a Billy Graham crusade constantly challenged herself and those around her to realize "there was never a life that God did not create." While today's culture has a system of judging people's importance by possessions, popularity, power, and position, from God's perspective we are all equal. She felt that in order to be prepared to reach out to people, "Our hearts must break for them. We must never stop weeping for the hurting."

One of the greatest ways to respect an individual is to help build value and self-esteem into him or her. Barnabus is an individual in the New Testament whose name means "Son of Encouragement" (Acts 4:36). He consistently built up the people around him. The greatest definition of an encourager I have heard is "one who pours courage into someone." Sometimes people simply need to be respected enough to have someone pour courage into them. Spoken words of encouragement and even small acts that show people they are valuable to you and to society can have a huge impact on their life.

Remember too that basic respect begins by recognizing that many needy individuals have a strong personal relationship with Christ that helps them survive day to day—resulting in a love for him stronger than many of those who are wealthy. Do not assume just because someone is poor that he or she does not know Jesus. People can easily read the attitude in which you approach them, and it can open or shut doors of relationship leading to ministry.

As the index finger can point the direction to be traveled, *building relationships* with those you are reaching is imperative for truly impacting their lives with long-term and even eternal effects. One visit can help temporarily fill someone's stomach, but it does not build relationships or open a door for really ministering to someone's life.

As you visit with people, rather than trying to immediately address their life and situation with advice, you need to spend time intently listening to them and their story. As you listen, put your life into their story and think about how they feel. Imagine their pressures of worrying about how to meet daily needs; where their child's next meal is going to come from; what it is like to stand in a line to accept food, clothing, and shelter. What is it like to always be dependent on others to survive in today's world? As is true with most people, you earn the right to be heard by sincerely listening first, seeking to understand them, and then finally speaking to them.

In the first pages of your Bible, during creation God states, "It is not good for the man to be alone" (Gen. 2:18). From the very beginning we see how much the Lord values relationships. Living day to day in need can be a very lonely place. As you visit people time and time again, you begin to build a very important and special relationship with them. Begin by learning and calling them by name, and then learn what is personal and important to them. Not only are you helping an immediate need, but you can become a friend who cares about the needs and the person.

The thumb stands for *taking responsibility*, which is necessary to make the fingers work properly. Jesus's own words and example command us and set the example for us on how to open the doors of ministry by caring for people. He has given us the responsibility to assist individuals. In Matthew 25:34–40 Jesus gives us the responsibility to aid those who are hungry, thirsty, homeless, naked, sick, and in prison as though we are giving aid to Jesus himself.

Service Evangelism

Jesus's ministry example was a combination of word and deed. He healed the sick, cast out demons, helped the blind see, and fed people. He realized that sometimes he had to help fill people's stomachs before sharing his message with them. We know more about how Jesus fed the five thousand than the words he spoke on that day. Sometimes people may remember more about how we help them than what we actually say. Helping meet needs is not an option for us but a responsibility from the Lord that allows all our fingers to work together.

When beginning to think about service evangelism, we start with the concepts of helping those who are thought of as *the least, the last, and the lost*. Service evangelism can and should also be a ministry-relationship strategy for the individuals we come into contact with every day. Some examples of service evangelism can include cutting your neighbor's grass or cleaning the gutters, washing a car, caring for a neighbor's children, or helping a friend when he or she is sick or in the hospital. These are incredible tools for preparing people's minds and hearts for when you have a chance to verbally share Christ with them.

Being part of the body of Christ makes us part of a family that cares for each other in times of need. For many not in this spiritual family, help from a friend or neighbor can be a new concept. When we took a baby gift and dinner to a neighbor who was a new mom and not in a church, she was surprised. This family did not understand why someone would care enough to take the time to help someone they really did not know. The experience helped a friendship grow that eventually led to the opportunity of helping them know how to have a personal relationship with Christ. Service evangelism can earn you the right to share Christ with both the "down and outer" and the "up and outer."

Be aware that there are some potential dangers of service evangelism. First, we can have *wrong motives* when helping people if all we are doing is serving in order to feel good about ourselves. One of Jesus's consistent challenges was to do everything with a pure motive from the heart and not a motive to be recognized for our actions. The focus of our service to others will reveal our motives. It is possible to help others visibly while inwardly focusing on ourselves. Our motives are false if we seek to help others in an attempt to make ourselves look good to those who are watching. Our focus on helping others must be on that person and his or her needs. Jesus challenges us to store up our treasures in heaven, not here on earth.

A second danger is that of *wrong theology*. Meeting physical needs without ever sharing the gospel is not how the Lord wants us to use our service opportunities. In Jesus's encounter with the Samaritan woman at the well, he says, "People soon become thirsty again after drinking this water. But the water I give them takes away thirst altogether. It becomes a perpetual spring within them giving them eternal life" (see John 4:13–14 NLT). While water for someone to drink is important, according to Jesus they will be thirsty again. His water of eternal life—spiritual restoration with God—will last forever.

Especially among a younger generation, there's a strong desire to *do something* with the gospel rather than simply talk about it. From collecting canned goods for the poor to mowing lawns, raking leaves, changing light bulbs, and building houses, there's a movement to *show* people what it's like to follow Jesus before *telling* them how.

There are, however, some potential setbacks to this trend in outreach:

It might diminish the message. The gospel is by its nature a message—Good News. If the focus becomes predominantly meeting needs, there is a danger that the deepest needs of the heart—forgiveness and life in Christ—may be left out or made a secondary issue.

It might be misinterpreted. If the goal of service evangelism is to verbalize the gospel, the very actions might be perceived as insincere and "bait and switch." A strong commitment of time and energy will be necessary to demonstrate to the skeptic that our lifestyle of service comes from the life we've received in Jesus.

—José Zayas, international evangelist and author

Third is a *wrong strategy*. If all we are doing for people is helping meet their physical needs, over time they can become dependent on our assistance and never learn how to improve their situation on their own. Minimally, in addition to meeting their needs, we should assist them in developing the skills and desire to help themselves so they will not remain dependent on programs or other people. Helping them physically is temporary assistance, but helping them spiritually has eternal benefits. While many of us may not be spiritually gifted as evangelists, we are all to be about the work of evangelism in the lives of people around us. If discovering a personal relationship with Christ is like climbing a ladder, we must be faithful to be a rung on someone else's ladder. We might not be the one to share the facts of the gospel and pray with a person, but it may be our acts of service that help plant seeds in someone's life that draw him or her one step closer to making a decision for Christ.

One of our long-term staff members, Mike Greer, coordinates all of our event physical arrangements, including sound and staging. One of his ministries is to employ day laborers as help on event days. He hires these men, talks with them during the day, and assigns them seating during the program. In almost all our events, some of these men make commitments to Christ. They come to earn a day's wage and leave with a new and personal relationship with Christ.

Looking at our full five-fingered helping hand, we see that our responsibility to assist others is made possible when we reach a specific need in a person's life, when we are real and authentic in our demonstration of helping people, when we honestly respect the individual we are assisting, and when we build relationships with them. Now we have one complete hand to be linked with the second hand of sharing the gospel with individuals.

The Second Hand

As we look at the fingers on the second hand, the principles of spiritually helping someone are the same as the first hand, although in a slightly different order: (1) taking responsibility, (2) recognizing a need, (3) being real or authentic, (4) respecting those who need help, and (5) building relationships.

Second Timothy 4:5 tells us to "do the work of an evangelist." Second Corinthians 5:18–20 gives us our assignment: "And God has given us this task of reconciling people to him. . . . So we are Christ's ambassadors" (NLT). An ambassador is someone who is sent by a sovereign to make friends on his or her behalf in a foreign country. Simply put, an ambassador is someone who makes friends in a foreign country.

As followers of Christ, we are in a foreign land, and it is our responsibility to share the hope and salvation we have in Christ with those who do not have a personal relationship with him. In order to be most effective with this responsibility, we need to recognize the need in the lives of others when they are without Christ. We can see the frustration, guilt, and unhappiness lived out by someone who does not know him. We must be real in our walk with him. As people come to know us as followers of Christ, they will watch how our walk matches our talk. If we are not real, we will have no credibility in which to share Christ. In fact, we will do more harm than good to the distribution of the gospel if we are viewed as hypocrites and used as an example of why the world should not accept Christ.

We must *respect* the person we are trying to reach for Christ. While we share Christ in confidence, Peter teaches us to do so with gentleness and respect (1 Peter 3:15). Remember, we cannot force someone to change. We must share Christ, pray for that person, set a good example, and have patience as we pray for the Lord to change his or her life.

All these fingers are most successful when realizing how important *relationships* are to evangelism. Once we build a friendship with a person, we have earned the right to tell him or her how it is possible to have a personal relationship with Christ, which is the ultimate relationship to meet our needs in this world and the world to come.

A pastor friend of mine has an incredible story of picking up a hitchhiker on the way to church. He felt strongly about helping someone because he was preaching on the subject of relationships. Driving along the highway, he passed a hitchhiker whose car had obviously broken down. My friend decided this must be it, so he pulled over and offered the man a ride.

Suddenly, my friend felt a conviction stronger than anything he had ever felt to share the gospel with this man. So he asked the stranger if he could share his faith while taking him wherever he had to go for help. He said it with so much passion that the hitchhiker agreed and listened intently as the pastor shared the gospel of Christ and how much Jesus loves him. After a few minutes, the stranger asked my friend to pull over. Then he confessed that the breakdown was just a ploy to get some unsuspecting individual to pull over and pick him up. The plan was then to take that person to an undisclosed location so a group could assault and rob the Good Samaritan. The stranger confessed that he could not go through with the plan and needed to have this peace that my pastor friend had shared about.

While this is a dramatic story, there is a direct biblical principal about being obedient to the Lord's prompting. Jeremiah was given a job, but he had an excuse not to do it.

> "Ah, Sovereign LORD," I said, "I do not know how to speak; I am only a child." But the LORD said to me, "Do not say, 'I am only a child.' You must go to everyone I send you to and say whatever I command you. Do not be afraid of them, for I am with you and will rescue you," declares the LORD. Then the LORD reached out his hand and touched my mouth and said to me, "Now, I have put my words in your mouth."
>
> Jeremiah 1:6–9

The Lord is going before us preparing situations for us to both help people and share with them. When we are simply obedient and follow him, we will help people physically and spiritually.

Since 1999 we have conducted summer Pathfinder mission conferences at SDEA. Our old format consisted of mornings dedicated to training students to conduct door-to-door evangelism. In the afternoons, students went out witnessing door-to-door and inviting people to come to evangelistic events in the evening. In 2005 we took 1,700 students to be part of one of Billy Graham's last crusades in New York City. It was an experience of a lifetime.

The following year we had a similar Pathfinder planned for Orlando, Florida. Prior to the trip, Hurricane Katrina struck New Orleans. The aftermath of destruction immediately became a focus of many mission trips. We lost 90 percent of our Pathfinder attendance, mostly to groups taking mission trips to New Orleans and other hurricane-stricken communities along the Gulf Coast.

As we look to plan future Pathfinder events, we will take what we learned from the Christian response to Katrina and focus more on combining service and evangelism. To attract individuals to be part of evangelism, we must first realize people today want to be part of an experience and not just an event. Second, they are more motivated by a felt need first and a spiritual need second. Finally, in our culture today of microwaves, fast food, and instant messaging, people want to see immediate impact in our ministry opportunities. While the presentation of the gospel will always be at the heart of our ministry, works of service need to become an important aspect of earning the right to present the gospel.

With many evangelistic ministries today, we have become too predictable. Our materials, programmed events, and even personal invitations to friends often do nothing more than remind them of their church services in years past. Evangelism in the days ahead will be more effective if we are doing unexpected things to get people's attention, such as unique activities of serving others without strings attached. A church in my community recently went to the local recreation fields filled with families watching children play baseball and soccer. Church members spent the day simply handing out free bottles of water and hot dogs. Many were suspicious, anticipating a "catch" of some kind. This simple gesture of kindness caught people off guard enough to make them curious about the church and check it out.

Being the hands of Christ to those we come in contact with is most effective when we use both hands: the hand to help meet people's physical needs and the hand to share the gospel with them. Two hands working together can fill stomachs and hearts.

We are to be Christ's hands and feet in the world, going to places where we can show Christ's love by meeting people's needs—and so earn the right to tell them about Christ.

5

The Nonnegotiable

Prayer

> When there is much prayer, there is much power. When there is little prayer, there is little power, and when there is no prayer, there is no power.
>
> —C. H. Spurgeon

Abraham was getting old—127 years old—and his promised son Isaac was still unmarried and childless. Abraham knew his son needed a wife, and it couldn't be just anyone. It had to be a woman from his home country; it had to be one of his own relatives. The problem was that Abraham and Isaac lived in Canaan, and Abraham could not make the journey to Israel himself. Instead he asked his most trusted servant to go and find Isaac a wife. This valued friend and employee knew the significance of his task. Before he left, the servant asked questions in order to understand the requests. Then he set off on his journey.

When he came to the town of Nahor, he stopped at the town well and prayed,

> O LORD, God of my master Abraham, give me success today, and show kindness to my master Abraham. See, I am standing beside this spring, and the daughters of the townspeople are coming out to draw water. May it be that when I say to a girl, "Please let down your jar that I may have a drink," and she says, "Drink, and I'll water your camels too"—let her be the one you have chosen for your servant Isaac.
>
> Genesis 24:12–14

Before he even finished his prayer, Rebekah came to the well and fulfilled the sign he had asked of God, down to the last detail.

I'm sure the servant went home to Abraham and Isaac with a smile on his face. After all, God had answered his prayers. The servant had fully accomplished his mission.

A Prayerful Foundation

If opportunities of evangelism are thought of as a *mission*, we should follow this servant's example by beginning our mission with prayer. By praying for the Lord to guide us in a special way, we lay a steady foundation for success in evangelism.

Our evangelist models have shown us how important prayer is to successful ministry. Billy Graham is famous for saying, "The three most important things you can do to prepare for a crusade are to pray, pray, and pray." Those were not just idle words but pleas to communities from his heart. Charles Spurgeon is quoted as saying, "Where there is much prayer there is much power, where there is little prayer there is little power, when there is no prayer there is no power."

If we believe in the importance of prayer in our ministry opportunities, why do we many times treat prayer as a last resort rather than a first option? As I think back to the greatest challenges in our years in ministry at Scott Dawson Evangelistic Association, whether it be finances, local ministry partnerships, even weather, those seem to be the times we communicated to the Lord through prayer with the greatest sense of urgency and passion. Imagine the power if we prayed as intensely for people to discover a relationship with Christ as we pray when we encounter challenges.

> Many evangelism strategies assume prayer support for both the speaker and the hearer, but far too often that assumption is incorrect. Not only is consistent prayer difficult to maintain in general, but it is even more so when we engage the enemy through prayer for unbelievers.
>
> —Dr. Chuck Lawless,
> Billy Graham School of
> Missions, Evangelism, and
> Church Growth

Charlie Riggs created and then for decades directed the counseling and follow-up program for the Billy Graham Evangelistic Association. Each Monday morning during the five weeks of the counselor training course, he met with instructors to preview the week's material. He began the time with the challenge, "I hope you are praying. If not, then you are on your own." We do not want to be on our own when sharing the gospel, whether one-on-one or with large crowds.

In many churches the only service that is less attended than an evangelism training course is a service devoted to prayer. Why would we dare to go into evangelism without prayer? Maybe we have the wrong approach to prayer. Prayer is simply communication with God. It is a main way that we grow in our friendship and fellowship with Christ. We would not approach a family member or friend only when we need something, but too often that is the only time we pray.

Do You Believe in Prayer?

How effective do we feel our prayers really are? Do they get out of the room in which we are praying? Why do we even have this question regarding prayer? Maybe we have been disappointed in how we feel our prayers have been answered and are hesitant to pray again.

We have a responsibility in how we approach the Lord in prayer: "The LORD is far from the wicked, but he hears the prayer of the righteous" (Prov. 15:29). When our relationship with Christ or others is stale or not right, this can greatly interfere with our prayer life. The most miserable people are Christians who are not growing in their walk with Christ. Communication, or prayer, is difficult when the walk is not smooth. Maybe we do not have confidence in the power of prayer because we have not put it into action and witnessed its results.

To overcome our questions about the effectiveness of prayer, we must examine our focus of praying. Are we seeking his hand or his face? Seeking his hand is simply taking our requests to the Lord. If we do not get our desired answers, we tend to be disappointed. If we are seeking his face, we want a relationship with him and trust him for the answers.

Evangelism is not an area to enter without serious prayer, yet there must be a balance in our prayers and dependency on God. There are many Scripture verses that instruct us to rely on God's sovereignty as well as others urging us to action. It is with this balance in mind that St. Augustine challenges us to pray like it is all up to God and work like it is all up to us. This is the combination that works to open doors of people's hearts to Christ.

Nehemiah is a great person to watch in prayer. He had the responsibility of being the king's cupbearer; it was his task to test the king's food and drink for poison or other tampering by his enemies. Through faithful service to the king, Nehemiah found favor with him. As Nehemiah learned of the disgrace and trouble being experienced by those living in Jerusalem as a result of the protective wall being in rubble, he wept, mourned, fasted, and prayed about what to do. After much prayer, he made a plan and approached the king to request not only a leave of absence to help rebuild the wall but also protection and provisions for doing the work. As a result, Nehemiah led the successful effort to rebuild the walls and gates around Jerusalem in just fifty-two days. As we consider the challenge to rebuild the wall around Jerusalem, we see that in order of importance Nehemiah prayed, planned, and then proceeded.

Prayer is where we need to begin. I have been in many prayer meetings, even regarding evangelism, where the prayers were very general, like "Lord, bless this event." I am thankful that the Lord can and does bless events. Much more exciting and powerful, however, is when we see specific prayer receive specific answers.

Billy Graham tells the story of a summer Friday night at a crusade in Columbia, South Carolina. The weather was terrible that night, yet thousands attended. At one point just before the service was to begin, the storm turned into a dangerous hailstorm and the nearly full stadium had to be evacuated. As the storm ended, almost everyone returned from either the stadium concourse or their vehicles. The program started and ran as planned until the moment Billy Graham was to begin to preach. The storm returned, this time with lightning. Billy Graham simply read John 3:16, explained it for about two minutes, and gave the invitation. Amazingly, over 1,000 individuals came forward to make a commitment to Christ. Those who came forward during the invitation could not have been simply responding to the words spoken by Billy Graham; he only spoke for three minutes. The power came from the hundreds of people who had spent time praying for friends and then invited them to attend the service as their guests. Prayer had miraculously prepared individuals for a life-changing message regardless of the messenger (or the weather!).

As Nehemiah, after much prayer, put a plan together to rebuild the wall, we too must put feet to our prayers. As we begin to pray for specific people we hope will hear the gospel, we may need to work on our relationship with them to earn the right to witness to them. Maybe we invest time with them or help them with a project and, in doing so, have the opportunity of seeing our prayers to share with them answered. Then we proceed. Once we have prayed and developed a plan, we must have the boldness to put that plan to work.

"Prayer Is the Undergirding of All We Do"

My good friend Michael Catt is the senior pastor at Sherwood Baptist Church in Albany, Georgia, and also executive producer of the football movie *Facing the Giants*. Michael credits prayer to the unusual success of the movie. He goes on to explain,

> With Sherwood Pictures the key is not technology, equipment, or promotion. We can truly say that every part of the process from script writing to shooting to editing has been bathed in prayer. As we walked through the process with all three movies—*Flywheel*, *Facing the Giants*, and now *Fireproof*—it has been prayer that has made it all happen. Someone who was on our movie set during the filming told me that what impressed him the most was that while we were shooting a very difficult and intense scene, a side room was filled with church members interceding.

We've heard from thousands upon thousands who have come to Christ because of the movie. We've heard from people on six continents. Many heard the gospel in their own language as the movies were translated into thirteen languages. I met a missionary from the Black Sea region who told me people were flocking to the church to see the movie. I received emails from people who were able to lead their friends to faith in Christ after viewing one of these movies together.

Often we are asked, "Why are these movies different from other Christian movies?" I can't speak for what happens with other movies, but these movies are made by a church. A long time before we ever thought about making a movie, we started an intercessory prayer ministry. Prayer is the undergirding of all we do. . . .

We want to change the world from Albany, Georgia. We are in a town of less than 100,000—a dying community—yet through movies, missions, and outreach to our community and our local Marine base, we are literally seeing God use us to change lives. Every week as I open my email and see testimonies of what God is doing in people's lives through Sherwood Pictures, I'm reminded that God *is* faithful; he *is* able to do exceedingly, abundantly more than we can hope or imagine. I'm believing God in prayer for the lost to be saved. It may sound trite or even simple, but it seems the more we pray for lost people, the more lost people we see saved.

How does prayer impact our personal evangelism? Prayer softens our hearts for the lost. Think of the individuals in your life whom you most want to avoid. Maybe you had a conflict

> Many evangelism strategies assume prayer support for both the speaker and the hearer, but far too often that assumption is incorrect. Not only is consistent prayer difficult to maintain in general, but it is even more so when we engage the enemy through prayer for unbelievers.
>
> —Dr. Chuck Lawless,
> Billy Graham School of
> Missions, Evangelism, and
> Church Growth

with them or a clash of personality. Maybe they hurt you or someone in your family. If you are sincerely praying for those people, it is impossible to hate them. You will look at people differently if you are investing time praying for them. Your heart will go out to them as people who are lost, and suddenly you will find them more approachable.

As part of our Pathfinder conferences we used to train students to share their faith and then send them out in groups of three to go door-to-door in nearby communities. One individual was designated to speak and the other two were to pray and learn. This kind of three-person team worked for Moses. As long as Aaron and Hur held up his arms, the Israelites had the military advantage and could conquer the army of Amalek (Exod. 17:8–13).

One of our teams made up of three junior high boys was walking down a street in Jackson, Mississippi. They went to a home, and the owner told them to get out of the yard. When they got to the next house, one of the boys said he had to go back to the last home, and he asked his friends to come with him. When they followed him back, the man in the yard exclaimed, "I told you to get out of my yard!" The evangelism trio left, but as they did, one team member left a tract and asked the man to read it. At the end of the street he looked at his friends and said, "We have to go back and try again." Can you believe this—a junior high guy going back after being rejected twice? When they got back to the house, they found the man sitting on a chair on the front porch—reading the tract. As the threesome approached the man, he looked up and said, "I was hoping you would come back. Would you please explain this to me?"

The rest of the story is that the man received Christ and then went inside his home and brought out his wife and two kids. All four members of the family received Christ that day!

Without this student being in prayer for the people he was evangelizing, there is no way his heart would have been soft enough to return twice to this man's house. Who knows if or when this man and his family would have ever again had a chance to hear and respond to the gospel.

For those without a relationship with Christ, there is spiritual darkness, but a small light can go a great distance in a dark room. Prayer softens the heart of the lost, allowing light to do its work. This softening is the supernatural work of the Holy Spirit that can take place without them even realizing it. I pray that God will place light in the paths of the people I encounter, using my word and deeds. He is the light of the world, and darkness cannot hide in the light.

In preparation for SDEA events, we encourage people to pray for very practical aspects such as good weather, program guests, and facility preparation. One of the specific things we ask them to pray for is family and friends who do not have a relationship with Christ. We leave a blank space on the prayer card for them to actually write several names as a reminder to pray specifically and regularly for these people as part of the preparation for evangelism.

Prayer softens the minds of the lost as God continues to speak through his Word. Romans 10:17 says, "Consequently, faith comes from hearing the message and the message is heard through the Word of Christ." Our prayer is that as people hear the message their minds will understand and be open to accepting what they hear.

Prayer softens the response of the lost as their hearts are warmed by the Holy Spirit. A friend of mine was scared to death to present the gospel to his employer. He was ready to quit and go on the mission field, but he could not find the courage to approach this gruff boss. The boss's language and constant barrage of ridicule had beaten this faithful believer down.

After many weeks of praying for courage and opportunity, the employee approached his boss at lunch. As he began to share his story, the employer would not even look up from eating his sandwich. My friend continued, but he thought his futile effort was about to be stopped with a tongue-lashing. To his surprise, his boss looked up and tears were streaming down his face. He asked my friend to continue with his story. By the time he ended his testimony, the employer was engaging him with questions and finally prayed to receive Christ. The prayers had gone before him and softened the heart of the lost.

Prayer for evangelism is both personal and corporate. Jesus said,

> And when you pray, you shall not be like the hypocrites. For they love to pray standing in the synagogues and on the corners of the streets, that they may be seen by men. Assuredly, I say to you, they have their reward. But you, when you pray, go into your room, and when you have shut your door, pray to your Father who is in the secret place; and your Father who sees in secret will reward you openly. And when you pray, do not use vain repetitions as the heathen do. For they think that they will be heard for their many words. Therefore do not be like them. For your Father knows the things you have need of before you ask him.

> Matthew 6:5–8 NKJV

Being consistent in praying for individuals to come to know Christ is vital to evangelism. Write their names down, and make notes of how you can serve them in building the opportunities to share Christ with them. Prayer of this nature turns us from being ministry spectators to ministry participants.

As important as personal prayer is, so is corporate prayer. Jesus also told us that wherever two or three are gathered together, he will be there in our midst (Matt. 18:20). When a group of people agree in prayer for a person to accept Christ, it gives all of the prayer partners extra strength and accountability. Those we pray with can check on us to see how the evangelism effort is progressing.

Friend to Friend

The most important part of what SDEA does to help a community prepare for an evangelistic event is Friend to Friend. This program specifically encourages individuals to list the names of friends, neighbors, classmates, and family and then pray daily that the Lord would allow them to be used to invite these people to attend the event. Friend to Friend is based on the example of Andrew; the first thing Andrew did when he met Jesus was introduce his brother Simon to the Messiah (John 1:40–42).

We depend on Christians to use our events as an opportunity to introduce their friends to Christ. Without Friend to Friend, the event is just a fun outing for church members; Friend to Friend turns it into an outreach opportunity. When two or three get together to pray for their lists of friends and family, we see specific prayers answered as these individuals make commitments to the Lord. Prayer allows us to become active participants in evangelism rather than just evangelism spectators.

A couple of years ago there was a television commercial for a discount airline in which a sales director hands out airline tickets to his sales force. They are speechless. The director says that in a day and time where we have become dependent on communication via phone, fax, and email, it is time to get back to face-to-face conversations and handshakes. In today's high-tech, instant communication age, we need to depend on prayer as the high-touch part of evangelism.

While methods of evangelism may be trendy, prayer still lays the foundation.

In preparation for a recent church event, we experienced the meaning of the phrase "silence is deafening." Members of all ages were encouraged to sign up for a seventy-two-hour prayer chain. In a day when it seems that louder is better, this prayer time in the church auditorium was experienced in total silence. Many members of all ages commented on how powerful it was personally to simply be quiet and talk to God. It was a "back to the future" experience.

Finally, as Paul challenges us in Colossians 4:2, "Devote yourselves to prayer with an alert mind and a thankful heart" (NLT). We need to be devoted to prayer for the things that touch God's heart: those who do not know him. We must stay in a thankful attitude as we pray for individuals to know Christ. We cannot force people to change, no matter how much we want to. We must pray for them, set a good example by the lives we live for Christ, and have patience that he will bring about the ultimate change in their hearts.

6

READY AND WILLING

Make the Most of Opportunities

If we do not learn from history, we shall be compelled to relive it—true. But if we do not change the future, we shall be compelled to endure it, and that could be worse.

—Leonard Sweet

A friend of mine is an outstanding entrepreneur who specializes in developing and increasing restaurant revenues. He was in Louisiana for business, and as the Lord would have it, he befriended a man who had opened a Thai restaurant in the area. The two men developed a friendship, and my friend wanted to help this young restaurant owner become successful in his new endeavor. For over a month they worked on a business plan as well as marketing and franchising plans for the new business.

One day when my friend was leaving to catch a plane, he asked the owner what he thought about Jesus. "Who?" the restaurant owner asked.

"Jesus Christ," my friend said.

"I don't think he has been in here," was the owner's reply.

"No," my friend responded, "Jesus—you know, the inventor of Christianity that has impacted the world."

The restaurant owner answered, "Well, if you think we need to serve it here, then I will learn how to make it."

The Attack on the Bible Belt

Although this story is humorous, it is telling to us about the state of the nation. This is not a man living in Thailand, Africa, or even England, but in the southern part of the United States—in Louisiana, the bastion of Catholicism in our country.

Could it be that we are so busy sending missionaries to win the world that we are losing our own country? In one particular southern city in which I was speaking to pastors from several denominations, one pastor said, "In our city of 1.3 million people, on any particular Sunday only 300,000 attend a local church." A pastor from another southern city announced that in his neighborhood there are more people at the soccer field on Sunday morning than in most of the churches.

The reason I chose to give illustrations from the Bible Belt is to make one thing clear: the "buckle" has burst! There was a time in our society that the three top keys to numerical church growth were location, location, and location. A church could be theologically weak, spiritually shallow, and intellectually challenged, but place the facility in an exploding community, and on any given Sunday people of that area would read their ad in the Yellow Pages and go join the church. Those days are long gone in America.

Today there are many thoughts concerning what is important for church growth. Some say nursery facilities give parents confidence in the church's ability to take care of the children. Others argue a strong children's program gives a child a foundation for the future. Additional church growth gurus say anything from youth activities, a strategy for teaching people God's Word, leadership development, emphasis on missions, and branding the name of the church in the community are essential.

Earlier in our country's history the church was the centerpiece for community activity. Everything from town hall meetings to school was conducted in and through the structure of the church. As cities progressed and more entities became increasingly influential, the church took a backseat in the life of the community. Then with a surprising change of attention, most Americans started looking after what and where their children were spending their time. The local school and the ballpark replaced the church as the central entity of the community.

The church continued to have its influence, but in most cases it was because the pastoral position was considered one of prominence in most communities. Reserved parking spaces and complimentary club memberships were given as perks to these local spiritual leaders. Through church splits, church scandals, and church slothfulness, the role of the pastor in most areas has shifted from one of prominence to one of scorn. I find it sad when a pastor does not recognize this shift happening before his eyes. There is a thread of our nation that still holds the role of a pastor in a high esteem, but for most in America it is looked at with criticism and even disdain. This convinces us even more that for the church to be effective in the next ten years we must be dedicated and intentional in the area of evangelism.

91

Commit to Evangelism

In the same sense, we must be committed to evangelism in order for it to take place. To reach people in this next era of life in America, we will need to have three key thoughts consistently in our mind: (1) be aware of our surroundings, (2) have an atmosphere of service, and (3) be available to the Spirit.

First, we need to *be aware of our surroundings*. I have a friend who loves to quote his own personal philosophy: "Wherever I go, there I am." It sounds odd, but honestly, it is a great insight. Most of us concern ourselves with where we want to be or have been and do not concern ourselves with where we are currently in life.

I was traveling to speak at an evangelism conference for a national organization. There was going to be over a thousand pastors in attendance, and I wanted to inspire, challenge, and equip all who were present. I got on a plane and spread out my notes to review before the conference. While I was studying, a man beside me began to ask some questions concerning my profession. I was caught between the need to study my notes and a desire to be friendly, so I simply replied that I was in the ministry.

"Ministry," the man responded. "Man, am I glad to meet you. I have had some questions that I do not know who to ask." Well, you can guess the rest of the story. I gently closed my notebook and began a two-hour conversation with my seatmate on the plane about a personal relationship with Christ. To be honest, I have probably missed more similar opportunities than I can count. Even on the plane, there was a sense of hesitancy because I needed to study my notes. How ironic that I was more concerned about studying my notes to teach evangelism than being sensitive to those around me who needed evangelism. Scripture shows that Jesus was a very focused man. But he never allowed his schedule to get in the way of people. I have never read where Jesus rushed through the crowd to get to another function. As you walk through today's schedule, be aware of those God places in your path.

Second, in order for evangelism to take place, we must *have an attitude of service.* Before you answer someone about what you do for a living, look at the question again. It is not, "What is your vocation?" Nor is it, "How do you make money?" The question is about what you do that makes your life worth living. This is not about being a professional or having a blue-, white-, or no-collar job. It is about the passion that drives you every day. Anyone who works with me knows how I conduct a job interview. One question always is, "What is your calling?"

I believe life is too short to just have a job. Everyone must have a job, but many settle for just that. Life is meant to include a passion that dictates every fiber within you. For a believer, life's passion should be making Christ known. Wherever I live, work, and visit, I need to be in an attitude of readiness to serve my Lord. In my opinion, we have allowed a small minority

---

In the greatest sermon ever given, Jesus instructs his followers to lay up treasures in heaven rather than on earth. He points out that wherever our treasure is our heart will be also. The question is, "How does one lay up treasures in heaven?" The answer is to invest in those going there. There are two investment accounts for heaven's treasures. The first one is the *gospel account*; we must be telling the Good News. The second is the *goodness account*. These two accounts work hand-in-hand. It is the second one I want to discuss here.

In Matthew 25 Jesus describes the judgment when he will place the sheep and goats in opposite camps. He then tells the sheep to enter the kingdom and speaks of the good things they did for him when he was hungry, thirsty, naked, in prison, and without housing. They are confused and ask when they did such things for him. He responds by informing them that when they did it for the least, they did it for him.

—Ted Traylor, Olive Baptist Church, Pensacola

---

of people to control the workforce for too long. The fear that most employees have about being a vocal Christian on the job is completely unfounded in light of the Constitution. We must be available to serve the Lord twenty-four hours a day, seven days a week, even during leap year.

The third key thought is to *be available to the Spirit*. There can only be one master of my life. It is either me or Jesus on the throne of my life. It is the same for you. If we want to be intentional in our daily life, we must be submissive to the Spirit's leading in our witnessing. The battle over faithfulness is faced in the private moments of our lives, well before we become public with our witness. Our own pride can derail us from being found faithful during daily activities. One of my favorite writers is Oswald Chambers. His classic *My Utmost for His Highest* has interesting comments on submission of the believer:

> A simple statement of Jesus is always a puzzle to us because we will not be simple. How can we maintain the simplicity of Jesus so that we can understand Him? When we receive His Spirit, recognize Him, rely on Him, and obey Him as He brings us the truth of His Word, life will become amazingly simple. Jesus asks us to consider that "if God so clothes the grass of the field . . ." how "much more" will He clothe you, if you keep your relationship right with Him? Every time we lose ground in our fellowship with God, it is because we have disrespectfully thought that we know better than Jesus Christ. We have allowed "the cares of this world" to enter in (Matthew 13:22) while forgetting the "much more" of our heavenly Father.
>
> "Look at the birds of the air . . ." (6:26). Their function is to obey the instincts God placed within them, and God watches over them. Jesus says that if you have the right relationship with Him and obey His Spirit within you, then God will care for your "feathers" too.
>
> "Consider the lilies of the field" (6:28). They grow where they are planted. Many of us refuse to grow where God plants us.

Our culture looks for authentic Christianity today, and real Jesus followers are kind to the hurting. At Olive Baptist we are investing in a ministry village that is designed to do the work outlined in Matthew 25. Our Charis House is a place we provide for women coming out of prison. Intensive discipleship is demanded, life skills are taught, and productive followers of Christ are built. This residential facility is an investment in women going to heaven. We see them saved and transformed by God's grace.

Our vision includes a clinic for free health care staffed with encouragers to share the gospel. Our Goodness Ministry provides clothing and food as well as counseling for troubled families. When we meet the needs of people and do it in Jesus's name, we find they become more open to the gospel. We are unapologetic about the gospel; it is the reason we are here.

—Ted Traylor, Olive Baptist Church, Pensacola

Therefore, we don't take root anywhere. Jesus said if we obey the life of God within us, He will look after all other things. Did Jesus Christ lie to us? Are we experiencing the "much more" He promised? If we are not, it is because we are not obeying the life God has given us and instead have cluttered our minds with confusing thoughts and worries.[1]

Consecration is the act of continually separating ourselves from everything except that which God has appointed us to do. It is not a one-time experience but an ongoing process. Are we continually separating ourselves and looking to God every day of our life, every moment of our life?

History-Making Individuals

The intentionality of our witness is crucial in order for the church to be effective in the coming years. One youth minister wrote, "My students are incredible in every way when I am

95

instructing them or when we are all together. One problem we are facing is that the students seem hesitant to be strong when they are not together in a group." What I have found is that this statement could be repeated by other ministers in every area and with every age group. Everyone is looking for a leader. If you study history you will find that history is changed by individuals, not groups of people. Groups are great for pep rallies but not for revolutions. Revolutions are always started by one person whom a group of people will follow.

This concept has been shown to me over the last few months. As I write this, my city is in the midst of a spiritual revolution. There is still crime and mediocrity, but the small group of people with whom I have influence is in the middle of an awakening. It all started about four years ago when a friend told me of a radio talk show host who wanted to get serious about sharing his faith. When we met, it was immediately obvious that we had a kindred spirit. We made a pact: I would teach him to preach evangelistically and give an invitation, and he would help me with my humor. Honestly, I think I have done a better job with him than he has done with me.

We started meeting on a regular basis and then had him share his testimony at several of our citywide events. It was great to see God molding a servant. This man's approach to the crowd was unconventional to those who had been to seminary, but the impact was obvious. He was using his God-given talent to connect with people over the radio and in person, sharing the gospel to anyone who would listen.

Then this past January something happened that changed our lives forever. During that month our ministry sponsors a student conference with over 7,000 in attendance. Due to the high demand and limited space, we are forced to conduct six sessions spread throughout the city for the students to gather for worship and instruction. So a speaker gives six messages in one evening! We have a driver waiting outside one venue to drive the speaker to the next session where over a thousand more students are patiently waiting.

My friend the talk show host had graciously agreed to speak for us during the conference. While he was on stage giving his third message, his phone began to vibrate. Although the phone vibrated continually, he waited until he got off stage to answer it. Then he got the message that his youngest son had tragically drowned. As he was taken to his family, the conference was called to prayer, and consequently, many students confessed their personal sins. During that conference, hundreds of students received Christ while thousands committed themselves to be totally devoted followers of Jesus Christ. In an ironic twist, the final verse the speaker had shared with the students was John 16:33: "I have told you these things, so that in me you may have peace. In this world you will have trouble. But take heart! I have overcome the world."

The outpouring of love to the family was overwhelming. During the celebration service for the child's short but impactful life, the father spoke from his heart. Through divine inspiration, someone had decided to videotape the service in case those who could not attend wanted to see it. The message was close to infallible; words were not wasted, and the gospel was shared. That day over two hundred people made decisions to follow Christ. The video was then placed on YouTube, and it skyrocketed to the number one video watched that week. We were able to link our website, www.sharingthefaith.com, to the video in case anyone wanted to respond to the gospel from the video. Over 25,000 people contacted our website during that two-week period indicating that they had been saved, wanted to be saved, or wanted more information. Other stories began to emerge of friends who had gotten serious about sharing their faith. Businesspeople were discussing spiritual issues while conducting board meetings or having lunches that revolved around eternal life. Several churches showed the video during their regularly scheduled services with amazing response. The story is still having an impact on our city, our state, and hopefully our nation.

The reason to share this story is simple. There is a business principle that can be applied to this chapter: "Without sacrifice there will be no success." The thought of having something positive come out of something so horrific caused some to criticize this family, while others pitied them. Yet could it be that this family actually placed their faith and trust in the one who loves us and who desires that we honor him even in the midst of tragedy? I believe so. The apostle Paul had this mentality when he gave his motto in life: "For me, to live is Christ and to die is gain" (Phil. 1:21). He realized that he was not at home here on earth and that his life was of little value when compared to the love of Christ.

In America we are quick to think that we are already in the "promised land" spiritually. We have everything at our fingertips. Materialism is exploding all around us, which causes a severe problem in our mind-set, taking our focus off living for a better tomorrow because we are struggling to make it another day.

We believe all our problems will be solved if we just wear a certain brand of clothes, drive a particular model car, hang out in the country club, or afford that type of vacation. The concept of delayed gratification is foreign to most of us. According to financial radio talk show host Dave Ramsey, "We've been sold debt as a product by the most sophisticated marketing teams in the world, and they're called banks. We've come to believe that debt is a way of life, the way to prosper is through the use of a credit card, that you can't be a student without a student loan."[2] Once debt is introduced into our life, our focus is divided. Let me illustrate: Look at an object right now. Focus in and observe every detail you can. Now, turn your eyes and focus on another object doing the same thing. Got it? Finally, try to focus on both objects (without moving them) and see if you can still view the details. It is impossible.

It would be one thing if the impact of materialism only hit those outside the church, but we also feel the pinch inside the church. One big distraction from ministry is when a church must focus on trying to pay off debt. When I ask young ministers what the biggest obstacle is that they face, most of them reply, "How do I serve God and pay off our debt?" We must return to the life of simplicity if we are going to avoid being too busy to evangelize.

In the book of Philippians, Paul constantly reminds his readers to follow the example of Christ. Christ had a heart of humility and a life of impact. Where is our impact today? Could the two be tied together? If our impact is shallow, could it be the direct result of too much pride? "For me to live is Christ" tells me that everything else should be lower than my desire to faithfully follow Christ—to be his person in the boardroom and his man or woman in the living room.

Then Paul continues: "To die is to gain." How foreign that is in today's society. We are all about living. Former Surgeon General C. Everett Koop has a remarkable saying: "Americans live in a state of marvelous mortality," which means we believe we will always have another tomorrow. That is

I often hear it said that everything rises and falls on leadership. Leaders are extremely important, however we find that everything rises and falls on lordship. When Jesus is Lord, ministry and the gospel walk hand-in-hand. The *gospel* and *goodness accounts* allow us to lay up treasures in heaven.

Often I am asked why we do ministry evangelism. My response is:

1. Jesus called for it.
2. It is right and it works.
3. It is on the final exam at the judgment.

—Ted Traylor, Olive Baptist Church, Pensacola

not necessarily the case; one day will be our last. On that day we only have one of two destinies: we can claim the promises of God, be found pure in his sight, and hear the words, "Well done, thou good and faithful servant"; or we can decide to store up our treasures here and face the result of our choices.

The evidence that lies before me in my study from the surveys and interviews with hundreds of pastors brings me to the conclusion that the fiercest competitor of the church will not be a Middle Eastern religion or an economic tragedy; it will be the constant tugging of the church's mentality to focus on today instead of living for tomorrow.

This mind-set is portrayed in the Old Testament through the life of Hezekiah. After his battle against Sennacherib, he was thought to be the best king since David. When he fell ill and was near death, Hezekiah petitioned the Lord to add years to his life. Through the prophet Isaiah, God granted fifteen years to the life of Hezekiah. Here is where the point is drilled home. During those additional years Hezekiah had a son named Manasseh, who would later become king at twelve years of age. Hezekiah may go down as the best king, but his son Manasseh will go down as the worst king. Manasseh wrecked the country, so much that not even a spiritual renewal later on could repair the damage he had done. Here is the reason: Hezekiah stopped thinking about the generation that was to come and put all the focus upon himself. This is shown in Scripture.

In 2 Kings 20:12 and following, Hezekiah had just been granted fifteen additional years. His first act recorded in Scripture after this reprieve was to grant the Babylonian envoy access to everything the country had in treasures and armory— nothing else was hidden from their sight. (At this time, it was Assyria and not Babylon that was the Israelites' concern.) Afterward, the prophet Isaiah asked the king what he showed the envoy, to which Hezekiah replied in verse 15, "They have seen all that is in my house; there is nothing among my treasures that I have not shown them."

The choices of a man who had grown proud of his accomplishments and careless in his actions would bring severe consequences. Isaiah gives the declaration from the Lord by saying, "The days are coming when all that is in your house, and what your fathers have accumulated until this day, shall be carried to Babylon; nothing shall be left" (vv. 16–17 NKJV). He goes on to declare that Hezekiah's children will be slaves to the king of Babylon, who had sent the envoy. Instead of having a contrite broken heart, Hezekiah's reply is simply this: "The word of the LORD which you have spoken is good! . . . Will there not be peace and truth at least in my days?" (v. 19 NKJV). The full attention of Hezekiah was turned not toward the generation that was to come, but to himself. Again, when we fail to be concerned about those generations that will follow, we will no doubt fail the first prerequisite for leadership.

When a leader with this mentality arises, the people will follow, but we are losing the right mind-set of leadership in evangelism. The cost of evangelism is great, but the rewards are worth the effort. Proverbs tells us that we are wise, Jesus tells us we are fertile soil, and Peter tells us we are blessed if we are condemned for Christ.

Be Intentional

Intentionality must be forged in our churches for the days ahead. It could be starting a Bible study at lunch, initiating a student Bible study before school, or inviting a non-Christian to dinner in our home. Wherever or however, let's get the message of the gospel to our community. Intentionality involves having three distinct mind-sets: (1) intention, (2) preparation, and (3) submission.

First, to be intentional is to have *intent*. This may seem elementary, but it cannot be overlooked. It is true that some people have momentary success without intent: making a hole-in-one on the golf course, winning the lottery, or even getting to attend a special meeting at work without meriting it. These are examples of the old southern phrase, "A blind hog sometimes finds an acorn." But compare this mind-set to that of the world's best golfers, economic minds, and leadership gurus. There is a major difference. You may be lucky every once in a while, but a consistent pursuit must be present to be intentional.

The second aspect of intentionality is *preparation*. An army must be prepared and supplied in order to carry out its mission. "No ammo, no intent" is what one former soldier told me. You can have the greatest intention in the world, but if you are not prepared, you are not intentional. Intent deals with your ability to be aware of your emotions; preparation deals with your mind-set (thoughts). Being prepared in season and out of season is our command from Paul. When you are prepared for an event, it can remove anxiety or hesitancy about doing what you must do to be effective.

In our particular concern with evangelism, a third aspect of intentionality is *submission*. As intent deals with emotions and preparation with your mind-set, submission deals with your spirit. Most of the time, my biggest struggle with evangelism is not in my head but in my heart. Scripture tells me to be a witness. I have learned the necessary verses, but still there is a battle to share Christ on a consistent basis. Why? It is a matter of the heart.

Surrendering to Christ is the step of allowing Christ to be my GPS (Global Positioning System). A GPS will tell you turn by turn where you need to be in order for your trip to be successful. Once I surrender to him, Christ reveals to me the steps I need to take, the place I need to be, and the person I need to speak with to be intentional. I've never heard a GPS system tell me, "Good luck on this trip. I've got no clue how to get to St. Louis!" No, a GPS calculates the best route, uses the best time, and gives clear directions. When a believer submits to God's authority, makes good preparations, and develops his or her mind to be a servant, that person will be the very essence of intentionality.

The next time you get in your car and start the ignition, ask yourself if you are prepared for the trip. Do you have a plan? Did you prepare and fill your tank? Is your GPS installed? Then start thinking about your family, your friends, even strangers you are going to see on this trip. Have you planned on sharing Christ? Have you prepared by learning verses, packing tracts, or bringing books? Do you have your spiritual GPS (absolute surrender) working? Have you asked God to give you step-by-step instructions and a spirit of obedience? If so, you are about to embark on a trip worth taking!

Biblically, I look to the apostle Paul, who is one of my heroes of the faith. He had a goal, and he was very creative. His goal was to preach in Rome; he longed to be there to see that empire come to Christ. Now, he did not get there the way he thought he would, and to be honest, you will not either.

God has your life planned out—he has given you a Rome, but he does not give you step-by-step instructions. Where is your Rome today? Is it your life, marriage, or ministry? As you travel along life's highway, what do you envision as your final destination? This, my friend, is your Rome. Paul would not let anything except God himself stop him from following his desire. Remember when Paul wanted to travel one way but the Spirit called him to a different way? An interesting insight here into creativity is to submit to the leading of the Holy Spirit—to be more concerned about being found faithful in God's sight than being the most creative one.

7

IMPROVE THE PROCESS

Creativity in Evangelism

Christianity, if false, is of no importance, and if true, of infinite importance. The only thing it cannot be is moderately important.

—C. S. Lewis

How do you teach someone to be creative? Can you force a person into a boardroom, close the curtains, and force him or her to come up with a new idea? I have also noticed that most people's creative ideas are inspired by or updated versions of yesterday's models. A good illustration is Walt Disney, whom I greatly admire in the arena of creativity. A trip to one of his parks or viewing one of his earlier movies will make you agree.

I remember the first time my wife and I took our children to Walt Disney World in Orlando, Florida. It was hard to tell who was more awed by the parks—the children or the parents! The children were caught up in rides and fairy tales that were brought to life. For me it was about telling a story. Every ride within Disney World is a story that unfolds before your eyes. As a ride progresses, the passenger is introduced to characters, plot, and the gigantic conclusion. The painstaking detail for every part of his plan is enviable for most of us in the church.

One of Walt Disney's dreams was to build a community based on his hometown in Missouri. He had fond memories of his neighborhood, but he wanted to add modern conveniences. His creation became known as Celebration. If you visit this Victorian neighborhood today, it is as though you stepped back in time to the early 1900s. Upon a more careful look, however, you discover that every home is constructed with the latest modern technology. Apparently Walt again struck a gold mine by understanding what people want.

One by One

How can we learn from Disney's creation of Celebration? For one thing, we must be careful to look to the past because the future may be there. There are only so many ways to create an environment for evangelism. A prime example would be the days of crusades or open-air campaigns in cities across the country. Most agree that those days are over, but I believe the greatest days may yet be ahead. There is a stark difference between mass evangelism and evangelism to the masses. Although there may be many people walking an aisle or even saying a prayer, each one is important in the eyes of our God. Everyone comes to Jesus individually. From

Zacchaeus who climbed a sycamore tree to the woman who had an issue of blood and touched the hem of his garment, Jesus is aware of each person and each need.

Although each person must come to Jesus one-on-one, we discover throughout the New Testament that God honors preaching to the masses. Jesus began his ministry by speaking to a crowd while delivering the Beatitudes. In addition, Jesus often performed miracles in front of large crowds. Then, in Acts 2, when Peter addresses the crowd during Pentecost and three thousand people respond, it is apparent that this approach is part of God's plan to grow his church. From New Testament times to the present day, preaching to the masses has grown to even larger numbers. But now there is a buzz around the country that the days of open-air meetings are over. This statement was posted on the *Christianity Today* website on July 5, 2007: "Billy Graham appears to be the last of a noble but dying breed."[1] Yet a similar statement was also made after Moody's death, before Billy Graham's ministry exploded in stadiums across the world.

As you can tell, I am biased toward this style of evangelism, but I also want to be wise. The future of open-air evangelism will be viable only as it is retooled for the generation it is trying to reach, not for the ones who have already passed. We now have festivals that are springing up around the country with attendance sometimes passing the 100,000 mark. After the festival, something else will be refined to bring that new style of evangelism into the forefront. The point is that every time someone says they have a new approach, in most cases it is a revisitation and adaptation of something that happened years ago.

Many pastors responded to our survey by indicating that effectiveness in reaching people during our lifetime will revolve around new means of presenting the same message. One pastor in the Midwest said, "We must quit doing church like our fathers and grandfathers. . . . This generation is looking for a new twist in the old message." Another denominational leader responded, "Evangelism over the next ten years will look more like the first-century church than the twentieth-century church."

A youth pastor told me that his biggest challenge is to come up with something new each month. I replied that it simply isn't possible. Is our hope for the future of evangelism based on coming up with something new or catchy every thirty days? If so, we are in big trouble. There is no way we can compete with Hollywood. For one thing, we don't have the budget. I know God owns cattle on a thousand hills, but he prefers to sell his cattle for a long-term investment; Hollywood spends its money on the temporal. Instead of constantly developing something new, we should create a think-tank approach and surround ourselves with a group of like-minded people who can develop creative approaches to reach and instruct students. Instead of focusing on trends that come and go, we need to build a foundation that people can utilize on a daily basis.

Any effective strategy involving evangelism must be inclusive of a real understanding of this millennial generation. If we are serious about evangelism we must be very intentional in attempting to reach what is described by the New Politics Institute as being the single largest segment of population in the history of our nation. This is no time for today's churches to cross their arms and be stuck in a rut when it comes to creatively earning the right to impact the future. The membership roles of our churches, as well as the ages of our preachers, are getting older and older; we are becoming grayer and grayer. We must ask ourselves, "Do we have the courage to face reality? Do we have the courage to face the future?"[2]

—Dr. Jay Strack, www.StudentLeadership.net

An additional challenge to effective evangelism is that we often fail in maintaining balance in the Christian life. There is only so much we can teach and disciple people in a lifetime. You can spend an entire lifetime on one verse or book of the Bible. I believe this is what has caused some concern in theological debates. People get bogged down with little nuances of Scripture, and we then try to justify every position we take on a few verses instead of the totality of Scripture. I can take a few verses out of context and make my case for whatever argument I desire. Our danger, however, is that we get people off balance in their Christian life when we start to major on the minors. I personally and wholeheartedly believe in the sovereignty of God, however if that belief takes me away from viewing Scripture as my mandate to tell others about my personal relationship with Christ, then I have wavered out of balance and am focusing on proving my point of view instead of viewing Scripture as it is written.

So if we cannot teach creativity and there is a danger with creatively, and we have already discussed that there is not much new creativity in the world, why bother with a chapter on creatively? Because of the necessity of challenging ourselves to be ready to share with a searching generation the gospel of Jesus Christ. When Paul goes to Athens, he finds people who worship numerous gods. So when he presents Christ to the Greeks he speaks in a way they can understand: "For as I walked around and looked carefully at your objects of worship, I even found an altar with this inscription: TO AN UNKNOWN GOD. Now what you worship as something unknown I am going to proclaim to you" (Acts 17:23, see also vv. 16–34). We also are compelled by Scripture to tell all about the love of God. This chapter will try to provide the principles of creativity that will help you penetrate and influence society with the gospel. After countless interviews with some of the most creative minds in the country, I have discovered several traits that are common to people who possess creativity. I will pass these on to you over the next few pages.

Traits of a Creative Person

I have found that creative people are *always looking for ways to improve things that already exist*. It could be tweaking an idea or improving a working model for another use. There is an innate desire not to create something completely new, just to make something better, more efficient, or faster than what already exists.

Everyone knows that Post-it notes are those little self-stick note-papers that used to only come in yellow. Just about everyone uses them and love[s] them, but they weren't a planned thing that someone got the idea for and then stayed up nights trying to invent. In 1970 a man named Spencer Silver was working for 3M company trying to find a strong adhesive (glue). The new adhesive Silver invented turned out to be weaker than anything they already made, instead of stronger. It would stick to things, but since it was super weak instead of super strong it could be easily lifted off. No one knew what to do with it, but the adhesive wasn't thrown out.

About four years later another 3M scientist, Arthur Fry, was singing in his church choir. He noticed that the markers he used in his hymnal kept falling out. He remembered Silver's weak glue and put some of it on the markers. The weak glue worked and the markers stayed in place, but they could be lifted off without ripping the hymnal pages. Ten years after Spencer Silver invented his super weak adhesive, 3M started selling the Post-it Notes nationwide in 1980. Now they are one of the most popular items for the office and people use them in all sizes and colors.[3]

A second trait of creative people is that they *always have a burden to make something happen*. It causes them to get up in the morning and stay up at night. One leader confided that he knew the difference between a God-given burden and his own ambitious spirit: "When my first thought about an idea is anything but seeing someone come to Christ, I check my spirit." What this person is revealing is that we can tell the difference between an idea and a gimmick if we view the outcome before the process. Our world boasts of riches and fame, but these will disappear if we keep our eyes fixed on eternity.

What God births, God will continue to grow through the power of his Holy Spirit. A dear friend of mine, David Green, has been hugely successful in developing Hobby Lobby. He has a remarkable sense of calling upon his life. David would very quickly admit that God has called him to be a merchant, but I believe he is one of the most creative people on the planet. He would not consider himself a creative person, but the evidence proves otherwise. He has started several companies, has developed new forms of charitable giving, and has one of the most effective companies in America. David is the epitome of being creative. His one desire is to see the kingdom of God advanced. I asked him one day over lunch why he still works as hard as he does. He is already a huge success, but his ambition to start more stores and see the future is amazing. He answered, "So we can invest more into seeing God's kingdom advanced." His concern is not about making money for pure pleasure; rather he is storing up treasures in heaven. Creative people always sense that a burden of responsibility has been placed on their life.

Creative people also *have a mind-set that failure is not final*. Failure is a part of life, and the thought of not trying hurts more than failing. Abraham Lincoln had more failures than successes, but he will always be remembered as a man God used to change history. How about you? Are you afraid of failing? We all are. It is not that creative people desire to fail or even have the absence of that fear. Real courage is being able to look at fear and still move ahead. A personal exercise of mine is to consider the worst possible outcome of various options before making my decision. I can then compare it to the best possible outcome and see where the real danger exists.

So follow your dream. Be creative. You may be amazed at the tremendous positive impact you can have.

Where Is Your Rome?

There also exists *an entrepreneurial spirit* in creative people. They like to row their own boat, dance to their own beat, and make their own path in life. Yet most creative people can place those desires aside when they are presented with a challenge or goal that causes them to partner with other creative people. Such was the case with Ray Kroc. Already an innovative thinker and successful entrepreneur, he grasped an opportunity to build on the success of two other businessmen with whom he had a working relationship. These businessmen, creative in their own right, had the work ethic to develop ideas into actual product. They laid the foundation of the most successful fast-food chain in history. But it took Ray Kroc, whose company supplied these men with milkshake machines for their restaurant, to build on that foundation and make their dream of expansion a reality. For as forward thinking as these gentlemen were, their skills were in the nuts and bolts of a one-restaurant operation, not in leading the franchising empire we all know as McDonald's. Gifted with great vision and practiced leadership skills, Ray Kroc was able to see the glimmer of promise hiding in Dick and Maurice McDonald's philosophy and turn it into the Golden Arches. His eyes were open to find the creative opportunities of his everyday occupation, and together with a lot of self-sacrifice and hard work, he was able to take something good and make it great.[4]

Finally, I have found that creative people are *not squeezed into one form.* This is true in every sense of the word. I have tried to find common traits about study habits, social habits, even sleep habits but have come up short. The only conclusion I have is that they are as different as snowflakes falling on a crisp winter's morning. Some sleep eight hours, others only five. Some take an hour a day to find their creative niche, while others enjoy a hectic life and can only find energy to move forward through interaction with others. I hope this sounds freeing to you about your own schedule and ability to be creative. Instead

It is time for us to realize we must earn the right to be heard. The Millennial Generation is very concerned about several things, including: Are we attempting to merely exist as a denomination or as a local congregation? Or, do we genuinely care about the hurting in our neighborhood and around the world? Research reveals that they desire their church to be driven to better the world globally, to be relationally authentic, and to be biblically focused. This is why the Student Leadership University experience teaches emerging young leaders to be very involved in feeding the poor, providing shoes for the needy children of the world, creating clean water, and providing shelter. They are deeply moved by the AIDS epidemic sweeping Africa, and they are up in arms about what has happened to the environment.

—Dr. Jay Strack,
www.StudentLeadership.net

of trying to imitate someone else, be yourself, sharpen your skills, and try to fine-tune what makes you more productive and creative in your own life.

This freedom to explore your own creativity will be extremely helpful as you seek to deepen your effectiveness in evangelism. Personally, being myself helped me understand my role as an evangelist. Most people think of an evangelist as a speaker who travels the world, and that is partly true. But I do not want to think of myself as just a "platform guy"; I want to be flexible enough to effectively address the current needs. Allow me to explain. In the early 1900s, the railroads were the mechanism for travel and shipping across the country. In essence, they had a monopoly. As society advanced, however, the railroads did not advance. There was a window of opportunity for the railroad executives to say, "We are not a railroad company but a tool for travel and shipping." If so, it would have opened the company up for airlines, trucks, and other forms of travel. The tools people use to travel and ship materials have changed over the years, and the railroad companies were not willing to change.

Methods Change, Principles Do Not

Evangelism is changing quickly around us in society. I have decided that I am not just a platform evangelist. My biblical view on evangelism is that it is a gift to be used by the church. An evangelist is someone who *strategically* plans how the message of the gospel is presented to society with the goal of seeing new converts assimilated into the local body of believers. My methods will change as society does, but my principles will remain the same.

Several times the ministry I lead has been labeled as *creative*. I would not want to argue that case, but we do have a strong desire to impact this generation. There is not a given formula for us to come up with a creative approach to evangelism. I learned early in my ministry that if you can't be smart, be quick to the idea. I hear great ideas all the time from people who never attempt to make them a reality. It is a shame to have them wasted, so some of those have been molded into our ministry.

Other ideas come by simple observation. I was at my son's Little League team baseball party several years ago. The kids got to go to a professional baseball game where thousands of people filled the stadium. I had just returned from a crusade where the stadium had only been half filled until youth night. (God bless pizza and Christian music artists!) I was in a discussion with Tony Ensor, then general manager of the team playing in the game my son and I were watching. I asked him if I could go to the pitcher's mound and preach. He politely rejected my offer. Then, on a whim, I asked him, "If I bought out the stadium, could I preach?" He turned, looked at me in the way only a baseball manager can, and replied, "Scott, if you buy out the stadium you can do anything you want!" Bingo! An idea was born.

The next week I met with my executive team. What if we bought out the stadium, gave away tickets, and conducted a crusade right after the game? At first everyone thought I was crazy. How could we conduct a crusade moments after the game without time to build the stage, create the environment, and keep the crowd? I didn't have answers to everything, but a piece of the puzzle had been answered by the NFL. I remembered watching the Super Bowl's halftime show and seeing a stage assembled within mere minutes—complete with sound. "If they can do it, we can do it!" I exclaimed. It might not be as big or dramatic, but a stage could be built.

We decided we would discuss this with pastors to hear their thoughts. The reception from pastors was thrilling. It had been years since we had seen such excitement among pastors for an evangelistic event. In every city where we had been preparing for a crusade, pastors had met us with hesitancy and lackluster support. Here was a new approach, and they bought into the concept very quickly. We studied and found that the hardest day for the ball team to sell out was on Sunday afternoon. We negotiated a great deal with the team for all of the extra tickets they had for a Sunday afternoon game where only 1,500 tickets had been sold in a stadium that seated 11,000. We contacted Dave Dravecky, a pitcher who had been in the news due to a career-ending bout with cancer that had cost him his arm. Dave agreed to come and give a testimony. We had music by a local musician, and I was able to share the gospel. The event was eventually called Safe at Home, based on the invitation to meet me at home plate to receive Christ.

The day approached with mounds of excitement. Two radio stations had bought into the idea and were pushing people to the game. That Sunday we witnessed over 8,000 people pouring into the stadium. There was really no way to know what type of crowd we were going to have on that day. Lines for snow cones and hotdogs were thirty minutes, and the stadium ran out of bottled water. The most exciting part for me was during the invitation when hundreds of people responded—an overall great win for the day. By the third inning of the game, the general manager had me in a discussion about what they would do differently the next year. It was no longer a question of if we do it again, but how we were going to do it again.

The next year we added a top-rated Christian artist and held training sessions in advance for people to help us during the invitation. This time there was huge anticipation for the day. During that one-day event, over 13,000 people came to the ballpark—the second all-time high attendance—and close to 1,000 people responded to the invitation. At that point, baseball teams from Bakersfield to Binghamton started calling our office and asking us to come to their city to preach the gospel. (Well, not in so many words, but they wanted Safe at Home.) Pastors were energized with a new concept of seeing people gather for an open-air meeting.

People ask if we lose the crowd after the game. Most of the time the game becomes the secondary reason people attend. One time the game went into extra innings, and when the visiting team scored, the crowd erupted. They wanted the game over so the event could begin. Now one danger with a successful idea is that you may think you have found the idea of your lifetime. Safe at Home is just one tool of many that we have in our arsenal to share Christ.

Another means we utilize is www.sharingthefaith.com, which is an online tool that can teach people how to share their faith. This came into existence when I was burdened to see more people doing what I was doing. It was an introduction to me about the difference between addition and multiplication. Any one of us can only be at one place at any time, but all of us can be everywhere. I

As you pray, plan, and participate in service evangelism, you are not only opening the door to touch the hearts of those who are being helped but you are touching the hearts of the Millenials as well. You are earning the right to impact them in many areas of their lives. Remember the Chinese proverb, "The pipe that carries the water gets just as wet as the bucket that receives it." If we truly want to be passionate followers of Jesus, we must be "moved with compassion," as the Gospels so frequently state about Jesus. Let's sound revelry for the Millenials by not *telling* them what we believe but by *showing* them what we believe.

—Dr. Jay Strack,
www.StudentLeadership.net

thought, *What if every Christian could learn how to share their faith and then share it on a weekly basis? Weekly*, because some people do not meet new people daily, but almost everyone meets someone new weekly. We developed this online tool with a place for the user to write his or her testimony and have it read and sent back with constructive comments. Once the testimony has been revised, we have a tool that allows the user to send the testimony to everyone on his or her mailing list. This email is received with a nice header, a quick introduction, and the story of the sharingthefaith.com user. At the end of the testimony, there is the statement, "Would you like to find out how to have this personal relationship with Jesus Christ? Click here." This link takes the inquirer back to the website where the gospel is presented. Both the user and the inquirer get an email explaining the next steps, and the user is encouraged to follow up with the one who inquired.

In addition, we encourage those who fill out their testimony to use it on a weekly basis through an email. We document these results on the website. On average, over 1,000 people are using this website on a weekly basis. Again, nothing exactly new in the area of evangelism, but a change made to reach society.

Share Your Ideas

Here is a suggestion to get your creative juices flowing: share your ideas. I have given away many good ideas to various ministries. There was a time in my life when I was concerned with the fact that all of those ideas were mine and other people should acknowledge that. But I now believe ideas are part of God's plan for my life. If I hoard them all to myself, I will never blossom into what he desires me to be. For every idea I give away, I have room in my mind for three more. It is the principle of when you give, you really receive more than what you give. I have a friend whom I believe has a really good idea about church growth. Unfortunately, he is smothering the idea to death. He will never share his idea with anyone and only revealed it to me after he made me promise not to tell.

Why have an idea if you will not share it? When I share my ideas, it allows me to flesh it out with friends. The sharing process will either refine the idea or make me understand that it is not worth our time and effort. My board chairman, Doug Harris, a great businessman, taught me this principle within the ministry. He asked me to share my ideas with the board first so they could be a part of the refining process. When I started doing this, it freed me up so much that I now bring all my ideas to these people first before I share it in public. Do not be afraid to share your ideas. Be wise in the disclosure of information, but do not live in fear that it will be taken. If someone takes that idea and makes it their own, more power to them because it is about cooperation, not competition.

8

THE CHRISTIAN BUBBLE

Protecting Ourselves from the Lost

We talk of the Second Coming; half the world has never heard of the first.[1]

—Oswald J. Smith

A few years ago I received an invitation to speak at a student camp in Oklahoma. Being from Alabama, I had not personally been to the camp and had no idea the scope or magnitude of the camp's effectiveness. The camp is Falls Creek, and at one time in its history, one out of every three students in Oklahoma had attended. The camp houses over 6,000 students a week for the entire summer. I was scheduled to speak for two consecutive weeks.

In preparation for my sermons, I asked the director of the camp which night he wanted me to give an invitation. "Every

121

night," was his response. This is highly unusual in most conferences, but it was music to my ears. He shared the vision for the camp: it exists purely for the sake of evangelism. The charge for each student to attend the camp is miniscule compared to other conferences. The students stay in dorms that were built by participating churches. All across the campground there are buildings as unique as the church that built it. This is all done in order to keep the cost down so unchurched students can attend. The camp director explained the philosophy behind the camp like this: "If an unchurched student has three hundred dollars to choose between camp and an iPod, we are history. If we can keep the cost reasonable, the students want a week away from their parents, and the parents a week away from their child." This really makes sense. Perhaps this is one of the main reasons most camps nowadays cater to students from churches—since unchurched students cannot or are not willing to afford to attend.

The price is just one area of thought given to making this camp evangelistic. Every aspect of the camp is about introducing people to Jesus. The Bible studies, the activities, even the structure of the service is about students coming to receive Christ. Every night I was present, hundreds of students came forward to discuss their relationship with Christ. The point is that the camp is intentional about evangelism. In order for us to be effective in evangelism, we too must be intentional.

To be intentional in evangelism is not to be obtrusive. The responses we received suggest that intentionality is not a call to civil disobedience and militia mind-set. Our culture demands respect for individuality, and this is exemplified by the huge decline in door-to-door sales because of the signs in most neighborhoods deterring solicitations. The same is true with the church. The days of going into neighborhoods unannounced are quickly fading, and the future does not hold much hope of their return. Churches once engaged in canvassing their communities with tracts and surveys in the hope of discovering new prospects for their congregations. Not for much longer. Recently in one city a group of students who walked through a neighborhood passing out literature were given citations by local police because they were in violation of the "no solicitation" ordinance. Several incidents have occurred in shopping malls where students have been asked to leave because they were sharing their faith.

Mark Cahill is an evangelist who specializes in teaching people how to share their faith. He is very quick to point out that we are called not to break the law but to know the law and make it work in our favor. I have personally seen him in hotel lobbies, in malls, and in stores sharing Christ. One particular evening I was entering the NCAA championship basketball game where he was standing on the sidewalk passing out tracts. I recognized him and said hello. He asked if I had come to help him pass out tracts, and I hated to disappoint him. Honestly, I had been invited by a dear friend and was enjoying the fellowship before we saw Cahill. A sense of conviction came over my heart as I was challenged to be more intentional in evangelism—after the game! Seriously, I did talk to the people who sat beside me, but I knew I had to be even more intentional in sharing my faith.

That particular evening a police officer quizzed Mark about his right to pass out tracts on public property. I listened as Mark gave the officer a brief history lesson of the country (he is a former history teacher) and explained why he had the right to do what he was doing. The officer acknowledged that he was a believer and was just following up on an earlier complaint. He thanked Mark for what he was doing and told him to continue.

There is a rather unfortunate myth floating around that says evangelism is an old-school event conducted by loud preachers with shiny suits, big Bibles, and an even bigger "I wish I could be Billy Graham" complex. Nothing could be further from the truth! I can think of no spiritual discipline that should outwardly demonstrate the inward transformation more than to love and share life with those who are spiritually dead. When Jesus shares the story of the Good Samaritan—one of the most popular and misunderstood of all Bible stories—he is painting a picture of his sacrificial love. The Samaritan, who is the Christ figure of the story, is intentional about getting in the ditch with the man who is desperate and hurting. Others were unmoved by the pain they saw— a calloused heart leads to an apathetic existence. On the other hand, to see what others are not willing to see and in turn weep with those who weep is to be both compassionate and intentional.

—Brent Crowe, www.StudentLeadership.net

Beyond Students

Intentionality is also not about an age group. Early in our research for this book we discovered a trend in responses concerning effective evangelism. Most leaders agreed that effective evangelism over the next ten years would be targeted toward students. Some called it "a spiritual revolution," while others hoped for "another Jesus generation." When we delved into the principle, there was only one problem: it was incorrect. It is true that we are seeing our greatest results with students in the area of evangelism, but it seems that is the only age group we are targeting with the gospel.

What about other age groups? We put it to the test with a senior-adult luncheon in my home city. We prepared for over six months for this lunch, which included music and an entertainer known to that age group. I had the privilege of sharing the gospel. My personal prayer request was for one person to be saved. We had six hundred in attendance, and when the cards were reviewed, we learned there were seventy first-time professions of faith, each one over the age of fifty-five. One woman prayed to receive Christ on that Thursday and then died on Saturday. Forty-eight hours after receiving Christ, she saw him face-to-face. We decided to test it again in another city—and saw even better results. It was apparent that although we had leaders agreeing that evangelism must be targeted to students, in actuality evangelism could be effective when targeted at any group.

Evangelism is most effective when it is designed for the specific audience. Tailor your approach in evangelism to the crowd you are trying to reach—just be careful not to make it exclusive to students. Students get the most attention in this area, but it can be adapted to each age group. As a speaker, I must remember that the first rule of communication is that it is my responsibility to have my message received by my audience as it is intended. Successful communication lies within the receiver, not the deliverer. You can say one thing, but if it is received in another way then it was not properly communicated.

One example of this is how people may view salvation. Congregations hear that salvation is for "anyone and everyone." In many churches, however, most adults see only students and children receiving Christ. I took my daughter to swimming lessons at the local YMCA and asked the instructor if older adults ever take lessons. She replied, "Every once in a while they will sign up and come to the first lesson. But when they walk out and see the children in the pool, they turn around, go back to the dressing room, and never return."

Some adults may view salvation like this. They sense a need for a real relationship with Christ, but when they see all the students and children going forward, they determine that this must be for kids and will not risk the embarrassment of joining them. We must explain that salvation is for everyone regardless

So then, Jesus came not only to redeem individuals but also to put the body of Christ, the mirror of God, back together again. Each piece of that mirror, each culture, once reflected God only partially, but uniquely and brilliantly as only that piece could. That uniqueness also enabled people of that culture to experience God and worship him in their own special way. It is for this same reason that the uniqueness of each culture gave rise to its own unique, deep sense of lostness and pain when God shattered the mirror of God (Gen. 11:1–9). So in the same way, effective evangelism must effectively relate to the uniqueness of each culture so its particular brand of brokenness can be healed by God and become, once again, that particular culture's greatest source of praise and worship to him.

—Stanley K. Inouye, IWA,
an Asian American leadership and ministry
development organization, www.iwarock.org

of age, race, or gender. Singles, families, children, and seniors are all groups that can be effectively reached when evangelism is designed for them.

Isolated Christians

Well, what exactly is intentionality? Intentionality is defined by Webster as "deliberate: by conscious design or purpose." In order for evangelism to take place, someone must have a commitment to maintain a conscious effort to make it happen. One pastor shared, "When I was young in the ministry I had the opportunity to share my faith on a consistent basis, but now I hardly even know unchurched people. The passion I have about sharing my faith has been replaced by my job keeping me isolated from the very people I am trying to reach." This statement could be repeated by leaders in every area of church life. A committed Christian businessman said, "If I could stop being involved with so many committees and programs, I might have time to develop authentic relationships with unchurched people. It just seems like I am trapped in a Christian cocoon." If we are not careful, evangelism can take the backseat to some very good causes. Have Christians taken themselves out of an opportunity to make a difference in society?

No one would argue that Christians should be different from those in the world. We are called to be light in a dark world, but by becoming light, have we taken ourselves out of the dark world? Jesus commands us to be insulated from the world; Scripture repeatedly tells us to be separate. In 1 Timothy 2:19, Paul tells us that the great foundation is: "The Lord knows those who belong to him [and] everyone who wants to belong to the Lord must stop doing wrong" (NCV). But some Christians have now moved one step further. We are no longer insulated from the world; we have become *isolated* from the world. We now have our own bookstores, schools, gift shops, radio stations, and coffee shops. It is now possible for a believer to go about daily activities without intersecting with a single unchurched individual.

For evangelism to be effective over the next decade, we must focus on intersecting with the world. One word of caution on this subject: Christians must be

The level of intentionality demonstrated by the Good Samaritan involved time, energy, money, resources, and follow-up. His love seemed to have no lid, and this is one of the marks of a follower of Jesus. Therefore, as we navigate through a sea of digital chaos jumping to read every text message, running to check our online profiles, updating the world on our latest comings and goings, and only slowing down long enough to fall into hypnosis before a glowing screen, we must guard our hearts lest we become calloused and unmoved by the pain all around us. . . . And then one day an awakening will occur and we will discover that we have unintentionally become unintentional with the most important message ever to be told.

—Brent Crowe,
www.StudentLeadership.net

different. We know that one reason people are not receiving Christ is that they see no difference in the lives of Christians. D. L. Moody once said, "Out of one hundred men, one will read the Bible; the other ninety-nine will read the Christian." Others should be able to see our life as one completely possessed by God, not as a life that is still searching for answers.

A friend of mine used a great—although very graphic—illustration about the dangers of letting the world infiltrate your life. His children were of the age when the world was offering some things that were inconsistent with the family's Christian beliefs. During a family discussion centered on how much a Christian should be different from others, the father asked if the children loved brownies. With a unanimous agreement over the love for brownies, the father asked if the discussion could continue later after some time to think.

The father baked a fresh batch of brownies and asked his children to join him and their mother in the kitchen for a taste of the chocolate delight. As the father cut the brownies, he asked how much the world would need to affect their life before they noticed. The children could not answer the question. The father then illustrated with an example of the brownies. He told them he had walked into the yard and scooped a little part of the puppy's waste and placed just a touch of it into the brownie batch. To the resounding sounds of disgust and even nausea, the father asked if anyone would like to eat the brownies. One child says that to this day he cannot eat a brownie without thinking of that poignant illustration, but they each understood the point that even a small infiltration of sin could destroy their life.

Christians do not need to be afraid of the world, but we must be aware; not scared, but conscious of the dangers of the world. When we have this perspective, we can be unleashed to change the world around us.

"Aren't You Glad Someone Told You?"

One pastor said that he had been led to believe evangelism was out-of-date until he was confronted on his own conversion. Someone asked him, "How did you become a believer?" The pastor replied that when he was a young boy, the Sunday school teacher led the class in a prayer. He received Christ and had never been the same. "Aren't you glad someone told you about Christ?" was the person's response. The pastor admitted that he had perceived that he was not needed in evangelism, but now he realized he was mistaken.

The other end of the spectrum is to think it all rides on your shoulders. There is one Christian school of thought that places the entire result on how well you communicate or on the verses you choose to share. This too is a very dangerous place to visit in evangelism. Luke 10 tells of when Jesus sent out seventy people whom he had commissioned. When they returned he told them he had seen Satan fall as lightning from heaven. He told them to rejoice, not in the results of their evangelism efforts, "but rejoice that your names are written in heaven" (v. 20). How could these men take any credit for Satan falling if they could do nothing to have their name written down in heaven? It is all a work of God.

So how do we reconcile the sovereignty of God and the responsibility of humans? When Charles Spurgeon was asked that question he replied, "There is no need to reconcile friends." We will never know the intricate details of how God works until we appear before him. In fact, if a finite mind can explain every detail about an infinite God then something is wrong. Don't get bogged down in the details; let's just take care of the task before us.

Not only should we be focused, we also should be forthright—ready to give a succinct and direct explanation of the gospel. I am afraid that many Americans think we should not talk about Jesus. My son returned home from school one day and told me a friend was asking him questions about Jesus. My son told his friend he would like to share Jesus with him, but he would call him that night because he did not want to break the law. "Break the law? What law would you be breaking?" was my response. "Dad, you of all people should know that we can't share Jesus in school," he answered. He had perceived with all the talk about religion in schools that he could not share anything about Jesus in a public school. I wonder how many believers think the same thing. When I explained his rights, not only was he thrilled, but he began actively sharing his faith from that moment until today.

What Would This Look Like?

In order to be intentional in evangelism, we must be focused on the task before us. I recommend that before you get out of bed in the morning you surrender the day to the Lord. Ask him to give you opportunities to share him in everyday situations. My family doctor is an inspiration to me in this department. Every day he asks the Lord to use him to advance God's kingdom. He and his family are on a mission with Christ wherever they are that day. I was scheduled for an appointment with him one afternoon when he walked in with an intern. I noticed the questions my doctor was asking were not like the ones we usually discuss. It finally hit me that the doctor was asking questions that would lead me into sharing my faith with the intern. I am a slow learner, but I finally came around, and within moments the two of us had led the intern to Christ. I had not realized that my friend had been sharing with this young student for several days and was dedicated to bring this person to Christ. I have watched this doctor cry over people who have rejected Christ and plead with others to receive Christ. The Bible tells us that they who sow in tears shall reap with joy. One reason we are not seeing a difference is that we are trying to see people saved with smiles, without weeping over their souls before God.

Let's be clear: no person saves another. God is the Lord of the harvest, and we are called to be workers in the field. There is an increasing argument among Christians that we should not take any credit for anything achieved in the Christian life. But we need to make a distinction between taking credit and being a part of the task. I am leery of any believer who thinks the Christian life is about us being like Christ but who leaves the privilege of being a witness for Christ out of their daily activities. If we are so confident in God's sovereignty that we are not burdened for our friends, neighbors, and fellow citizens to share the greatest message of Christ, then something is wrong.

Another misconception is that Americans do not want to speak about their spiritual condition. The old adage that religion and politics are two things that should never be discussed rings in most of our ears. I believe those are the two topics that should be discussed the most, but that is another topic. I still battle those thoughts when I sit in a plane or meet someone new. Why do we feel like this? We possess the greatest hope this world could experience, yet our lips are like concrete when the opportunity comes our way to share Christ. I have even started a conversation in my head while sitting next to someone. In this imaginary discourse, I share Christ only to be rejected. Talk about a pessimist. Sometimes we feel it is almost impossible to see someone come to Christ. It is possible, however, that we have come to believe the mind-set of "live and let live" in this society as well as "Americans just want to have fun."

Evangelism will be effective when it targets each fragment of the mirror of God. Genesis 1:26 relates that God said, "Let us make man in our image, in our likeness." Who is the *us* in this passage? The Trinity—Father, Son, and Holy Spirit. God created us—humanity—not only to reflect him as individuals but, together, to be like a giant, global-size mirror that fully reflects him. The body of Christ concept originated at creation. We were to be like a mammoth, full-length mirror reflecting our Creator. We were to be like Jesus, a physical manifestation of all the invisible attributes of the Trinity.

Then, through the Tower of Babel incident recorded in Genesis 11, we messed everything up by trying to make a name for ourselves—our own identity separate from God. We tried to build a monument reaching to the heavens that would symbolize the power of a united humanity without God. The tower was like a giant exclamation point that declared our independence—the building of the kingdom of humans instead of the kingdom of God. So God said, "Come, let us go down and confuse their language so they will not understand each other" (Gen. 11:7). Once again God refers to himself as "us," and he does what is necessary to stop humans. The Trinity scatters humanity to the ends of the earth and causes us to speak different languages. The mirror of God was shattered and all the cultures of the world were born that day—each culture but a broken, jagged, foggy, distorted, and dislocated piece of a once glorious and glorifying whole that fully and completely reflected God in his entirety.

—Stanley K. Inouye, IWA, www.iwarock.org

Look at any commercial on television and you will see that life is very good. A mentality of euphoria fills the screen as long as you add some alcohol or friends gathering for a meal. When this image is pounded into our heads for hours a day, it is possible for us to come to believe it must be correct. Television shows never go beyond the surface. We aren't shown the breakup of a marriage, the DUI arrest, or the sleepless nights filled with guilt and the desperate search for peace. Do not get sucked into the mentality that everyone has their life together. Written inside the cover of my Bible is the statement, "Every person I meet is searching for meaning, wondering about peace, and suffering with guilt." With those topics continually before my mind, I will always be ready to speak a word about Christ.

In conclusion, we should be prepared before the event happens. In his book *Seven Habits of Highly Effective People*, Stephen Covey describes effective people as ones who begin with the end in mind. The same is true with our intentional approach to evangelism. What could possibly happen when you share your faith? Could someone reject your approach? Yes, but how bad could that be compared with how good it would be to have the opportunity to see someone come to know Christ? Another outcome could be a discussion that leaves you with more questions in your mind than answers you have given to the one with whom you were discussing Christ. This outcome is nothing to be afraid of; instead it is an opportunity for your faith to be strengthened and prepared for future discussions. In every activity, be aware of those whom God has placed around you who are in need of evangelism.

9

No Lone Rangers

Partners for the Best Cause

In the past, a leader was the boss. Today's leaders must be partners with their people. . . . They no longer can lead solely based on positional power.

—Ken Blanchard

A couple of years ago *synergy* developed as a catchword in business. It is defined in the Collegiate Dictionary as "the combined healthy action of every organ of a particular system." The term then began to grow to include partnerships between airlines, rental companies, and even media services that started to merge and interact with each other to be more effective and efficient in their services. What seems strange is that this was coming from secular society and not from the body of Christ.

Without question, the greatest struggle for the body of Christ is unity. If the body would become unified in spirit, the gates of hell could not stop us. The moral failures of our leaders, the political infusion of our egos, and the materialistic mind-set of our lives are not as damaging to the body of Christ as the divided spirits among Christians. One pastor confided, "My fellow pastors would not waste their time to call and congratulate me for something positive, but they would crawl over each other if they could speak negatively toward me." This is not just true about pastors or clergy. A young professional told us, "I am bombarded by conversations with church people who want to argue spiritual issues. It seems like it is harder to get along with Christians than with my lost friends."

The division that exists has caused many in our society to lose respect for the church. One businesswoman responded to our survey by saying, "I love Jesus and have a personal relationship with him, but my co-workers do not attend church, and they have a negative view of Christians. I am afraid that if I told them of my relationship with Christ I would lose the trust they have in me." She felt that if she actually told her colleagues that she is a Christian, she would lose any type of influence she has in her company. This is a sad indictment upon the church of Jesus Christ. What has caused this lack of influence in our culture? How can we rebuild our influence in today's culture—or can we? How can we change the culture of the people we are trying to reach?

This chapter deals with the influence the church needs in our culture in order to be effective in evangelism. We have lost our impact in the everyday lives of most Americans. Os Guinness has a penetrating look at this in his study of Christian influence. I remember reading this in his unpublished study called "If Not Now, When?" which is a discourse on impacting the American culture. In the study he argues that we have never had so many

Christian leaders in so many powerful positions, yet they are producing very little influence in today's culture. He traces the declining influence across the country and concludes that we have lost all influence within the media and academic fields and our only remaining influence is within the political and sports communities. At the current rate, without working together we are in danger of seeing any influence through an outspoken Christian witness becoming extinct within American culture in the next two generations.

There is a major problem with any minister not willing to work with other ministers. I call it the "Lone Ranger" approach to ministry. I have never been attracted to this style and honestly do not know how it happens. When I think of the word *solitaire*, I think of either a silly game (that I never win) or prison. I never think of it in terms of the Christian life! Paul tells us to bear each other's burdens (Gal. 6:2). Scripture commands us to be one (John 17:11), which was Jesus's prayer for his disciples. Today in America, are we closer to or farther away from fulfilling that command than we were fifty years ago? I think we are farther away from unity, and that is tragic.

Influence

John Maxwell, author of *The 21 Irrefutable Laws of Leadership*, gives a succinct definition of *leadership*: influence. Without influence, it is impossible to lead personally, professionally, or spiritually. Influence is hard to acquire but essential for any level of success. You may not be able to draw a picture of influence, but you experience what it is every day. Just look at a room during a meeting. Wait until a crucial matter is being discussed. When the leader speaks, people will listen. You've just experienced influence. Again, without influence it is impossible to lead. The same is true for the church in our attempt to be effective and impact our culture with change for Christ. When the church has lost its influence in a community, how can it be regained? Or can it?

Yes, the church's influence can be regained in the community, but it will not be the same as it was before. That can be good. Dr. Crosby, the pastor of the First Baptist Church of New Orleans, walked through the storm, literally, when his church was destroyed by Hurricane Katrina. After all the catastrophic damage to the city and the incredible response from the church across America, he is still facing years of rebuilding homes, his staff, his church, and his city.

One day I was in New Orleans with Dr. Crosby, preparing for a citywide event. I asked him if he was ready for things to get back to the way they had been before the hurricane. "Absolutely not!" was his stern reply. "If things get back to the way they were, then we went through this for nothing. I want to see things continue to get better every day." This type of leadership is seen throughout the city of New Orleans as its leaders are committed to seeing change happen in their community.

I have observed the church's influence grow over the last few years in times of devastation in our country. In 1995 when the Oklahoma City bombing took place, the church was the first one on the scene and sent thousands of volunteers. After the terrorists' attack on 9/11, people flocked to the church. When the hurricanes hit, the first ones to respond were from churches. Why does this happen?

Ecumenism

Let's notice some trends that happen during a tragedy that I challenge you to apply in your community today *before* a tragedy happens: ecumenism, encouragement, empowerment, enrichment, and engagement. First, there is an ecumenical spirit. Neither the Baptist, Presbyterian, nor nondenominational groups will reach our cities for Christ in exclusion. When we reach over denominational boundaries, it seems to attract the attention of the community. A simple illustration is a splinter. A splinter by itself only brings aggravation and is a nuisance. If you connect thousands of splinters, however, you create a board that can have an impact. When the body of Christ is splintered in a community, we are considered an eyesore, but when we connect, we become a mighty force that dramatically impacts the community.

How open should we be in working together to impact a community? Well, in a tragedy we should be open to working with everyone regardless of denomination or theology to make our community better. It is not a time to wage a war over religious conviction when people are in the first stages of a crisis. When we are trying to make an impact on a city, however, there should be discernment. We shouldn't blindly work with every building that has a church sign out front. At SDEA we have realized that the secondary theological beliefs vary greatly, but there are two fundamental theological convictions that a church must hold to in order to participate in our events. First, the church must hold that the Bible is the infallible Word of God. We do not add anything nor take anything away. The second fundamental theological conviction is that

I would say two trends intertwine to reveal the need of the hour in evangelism today. First, we must shift from seeing Christianity as an institution we maintain to a movement we advance. Second, we must focus evangelism to be increasingly about what we do in the culture, outside a building. This includes focusing less on programmatic evangelism weekly or periodically and more on daily living out an intentional witness. (Note that in Acts the word *daily* is used nine times or more.) In so doing we must add without subtracting, for evangelism training and events will always be vital. We have tended to make them almost exclusive.

—Alvin Reid, Southeastern Baptist Theological Seminary

Jesus Christ is the only way to have eternal life in heaven with God the Father. There are no degrees to heaven, and there are not multiple ways to get there. If a fellowship adheres to these convictions, there is unity in making an impact in a city.

Why has there been such a change in churches working together in our communities? Well, beside theological differences, there is another reason.

I am indebted to Ernie Perkins who shared his insight into this developing crisis of lack of influence by giving a different view of pastoral competition. He was the director of missions for the Southern Baptist denomination for many years and has had a great relationship with churches of all denominations. His knowledge of pastoral diversity over the years is very insightful. He says the word picture of a pastor was once a *shepherd*. Sheep are in need of each other. The body of Christ loved together, served together, and grew together in what was called "the flock." The pastor was part of the flock. The shepherd loved the sheep and was deeply associated with them because the shepherd was also a sheep under the authority of Christ.

Today the terminology has changed. Pastors no longer want to be called a sheep; they prefer an eagle. This description is used widely in leadership training and with many church consultants. An eagle is very different from a sheep. An eagle is territorial, a loner, and as a sheep grazes in a field, an eagle devours its food. This description is intended not to offend clergy but rather to recognize that a paradigm shift has taken place in ministry.

Perkins's thoughts are derived not from mere observation but from engagement with ministers across the country. He concludes that most ministers are now being pushed into more of a CEO role of the church instead of a shepherd. As a result, a pastor is considered a leader of a publicly traded company;

the only things that matter are results and growth by whatever means necessary. The pressure of the daily battle to produce has caused many pastors to burn out or turn to other professions entirely. Pastors' experience of tremendous pressure could be attributed somewhat to the ignorance of the congregation concerning the role of a pastor. Pastors have told me that one of their biggest challenges is to instruct their congregation that the church is not a business and the pastor is not a CEO.

Encouragement

Tragedy displays the value of an ecumenical spirit; it also shows the serious need for all Christians to be an encouragement to others. Here is a tip: negative people usually attract negative people. The Bible says that bad company corrupts good habits, and I believe this also applies to attitude. If a church has a martyr mentality of reaching their community, it is only one generation away from extinction. This is not a lesson from *The Power of Positive Thinking*, but there are numerous Scriptures that deal with having a sense of enthusiasm or encouragement, including:

> So then we pursue the things which make for peace and the building up of one another.
>
> Romans 14:19 NASB

> Therefore encourage one another and build each other up, just as in fact you are doing.
>
> 1 Thessalonians 5:11

> Carry each other's burdens and in this way you will fulfill the law of Christ.
>
> Galatians 6:2

> Let us consider how to stimulate [encourage] one another to love and good deeds.
>
> Hebrews 10:24 NASB

Think about who has made an impact on your life. It is always someone who thinks the best of you, believes in you, and tries to help you get to another level. So it is with us as believers. The ones who really challenge us are the ones who believe in us.

The story of Rick and Dick Hoyt, the nationally renowned father and son marathon and triathlon athletes known as "Team Hoyt," comes to mind. Rick, a quadriplegic with cerebral palsy is pushed in his wheelchair by his father, Dick. When Rick was born in 1962, doctors had little hope that he would have a normal life. But his parents refused to listen and were adamant to raise Rick like a "normal" boy. At the age of twelve Rick learned to communicate through an interactive computer that required only slight head movements for different letters. When Rick learned of a benefit run for another individual who was paralyzed and needed financial assistance, he asked his dad to run. His father answered that he would only do it with his son. They finished second to last, but they finished. Now this duo has competed in triathlons and Iron Man competitions. The success does not end with athletics.

I gladly embrace the word *missional* as key to understanding evangelism in the future, especially in the West. *Evangelism* means sharing the gospel with someone; *missions* means getting to know a person's culture to become more effective in evangelism. We must merge these two in an increasingly biblically illiterate culture like ours.

Here is an example: For some time now I have asked congregations, pastors at evangelism conferences, and my students to raise their hand if they were raised in a Christian home. Most raise their hand. "How many of you remember your family ever talking about reaching your neighbors with the gospel?" Almost none. We do not even raise our children to give a flying rip about their neighbors.

—Alvin Reid, Southeastern Baptist Theological Seminary

Rick has graduated from college and works to help others who are paralyzed. This is a beautiful illustration of how life is not to be lived alone. Think about how others and even generations to come can be impacted for Christ when we focus on serving another person and stimulate them to do good works (Heb. 10:24).

Empowerment

Empowerment is the next tool alongside ecumenism and encouragement. If you are trying to do it all yourself in evangelism, this world will not be won to Christ. I have found that when a church, group, or person is making an impact in a place, there is a keen sense of empowerment among the followers.

A well-known evangelical leader confided in me that he believes that over 80 percent of the churches in America are declining or stagnant. A Southern Baptist denominational researcher told me that out of 35,000 churches in America, more than 20,000 did not reach four people for Christ in the last twelve months. How can over half of a major denomination's churches not see even four people come to Christ? Could it be that congregations have not learned to be empowered?

True empowerment comes from the Holy Spirit. Tony Evans, in his book *America's Only Hope*, says, "The power of the Holy Spirit propels the church to go beyond its walls and into the world. The Holy Spirit gives the church the power to be what God has called it to be: the visible demonstration of Jesus Christ in the world. It enables the church to minister to the world, and our ministry is to let the world know who Jesus is. If the world doesn't know Jesus, then we have failed."[1]

What would happen if we each invested our lives in two people over a twelve-month period and multiplied ourselves to see people come to Christ? I spoke to a pastor who had not seen one person come to Christ during his three-year tenure. He was quick to blame the community that had transitioned into crime, his congregation that was elderly and unconcerned, and even his own family, who would not share Christ if their lives depended on it. Finally I had had enough. I asked him, "When was the last time you shared your faith?" He did not have an answer. I challenged him to commit to share his faith every chance he got and to develop a relationship with someone in his congregation to train this person to also share his or her faith. If we are going to be effective, we must be training others and empowering them to share their faith.

Enrichment

The enrichment of others is the next element that needs to occur. It is one thing to empower someone, but you should also enrich the life of each person you meet. Everyone who comes into your life needs to leave a better person, and not necessarily better to serve you. In one year I had three executive staff people transition to other positions across the country. I was a little embarrassed but also hurt because of all the hours I had poured into their lives. Then a dear friend reminded me of a great point about enriching other people's lives. He said, "The only thing worse than training someone and losing them is not training them and keeping them!"

We discover our lives are enriched by enriching others. Occasionally I meet with young ministers who feel called into evangelism. They walk into the office with no clue as to what an evangelist does all day. They imagine an evangelist must pray and study all day long and then rise to preach to 10,000 people each night. An evangelist must pray; an evangelist must study; an evangelist loves to preach to 10 or 10,000. But there is so much more to an evangelist's life. Like every believer, an evangelist must earn the right to be heard. I relay the message that we are not in the *God business*; he is in business for himself. We are in the *people business*. If people do not respect us, we will not be allowed to share Christ with them.

It goes back to the missional approach to ministry that we have discussed. We are missionaries trying to find out how to engage a culture. Our first approach to ministry is to find out how we can help others and enrich their lives with the gospel. As a Christian, I realize that life is not about what I can get. I only deserve one thing in this world, and only by the grace of God will I not get it. So when I get Jesus, there is nothing else to get. He is more than I could ever imagine and so much more than I deserve.

If it is not about what I can *get*, then it becomes about what I can *give*. There are so many people in this world who spend their entire life striving for what cannot be attained and neglecting the very thing they need the most. Enrich the lives of others and your influence will grow.

Engagement

The final key is to engage others. In order for your influence to grow and the power of partnership to exist, you must engage in the life of another. Leaders are people persons; they love people. It is not something that can be taught, but it can be caught. In evangelism, you must be engaging people in conversations that can lead them to Christ. It makes sense then that in order to help people come to Christ, we must know how to approach them. Think about what new stories, friendships, or connections you can make as you approach people on a daily basis. If you do not feel comfortable talking about yourself (which is a rarity), that is actually a strength, because we need to ask questions about the other person. We must be aware of the individual to whom we are speaking. Take time to notice the surroundings, pictures, or anything else that can begin a conversation that can eventually be turned to things of God.

In the same sense of influencing our communities, these principles can help us get to know the body of Christ around us. As we have discovered, most church people focus on getting to know their congregation but feel isolated when they are in their daily activities. Pastors seem to feel isolated from pastors of other denominations in their city. In certain cities there has been some progress in these relationships through groups like Prayer Summits. Prayer Summits began in the Northwest and were designed to promote bringing pastors together with a focus on prayer. During this weekend, pastors communicate with each other and get to know the real person rather than the perceived person.

In a conversation with a prayer group from Knoxville, they described the importance of working together as pastors in their city. During one of the first Prayer Summits, two pastors were there who had never had a conversation but had been embattled with gossip and ridicule toward each other based on fiction and not fact. On the second day of the summit, the two pastors met in the center of the room, and one pastor confessed his malicious attitude while the other pastor confessed jealousy and a deep sense of competition between the two churches. As these two pastors embraced, the room erupted into applause. After this happened, the entire group began to buzz with anticipation of spiritual awakening and future opportunities in the Knoxville area.

We must remember the words of William Wilberforce: "A man can change his times, but he cannot do it alone."

10

Nothing but the Cross

The Good Old Good News

Evangelism is an important task and a vital role for the believer to fill. As has been said, evangelism is not just the task of the church, it is her very nature.

—Lewis Drummond

While I was in school, I had to take a class on preaching. I was fortunate to attend an evangelical seminary, but the preaching professor was not considered a conservative. It is one of the most intimidating times in a young minister's life. You must stand before the class to speak, and then afterward your fellow students critique you and give you a grade. After my diligent attempt to be the next Billy Graham was over, I was somewhat pleased with the remarks from my fellow student expositors.

What did surprise me, however, were the closing remarks from my professor.

The professor informed me, "You will be a good preacher one day, but you might as well resign yourself to be in far, out-of-the-way places because you preach about the blood and the cross too much." First, I hope he buys this book. Second, you can't always script a response to a critic, let alone a response to someone in authority over you. I did not remember what I said until a friend reminded me outside the classroom. He said my response to the professor was, "You have given me the greatest compliment a preacher could ever receive." I still believe that to this day. If we take the message of the cross and blood out of the gospel message we have today, we will reduce ourselves to giving fireside chats to bored congregations.

Watered-Down Theology Creates Weak Believers

The one clear message I have received from our research is that there has been an abundant, but not exclusive, amount of watered-down theology presented across the country. This weak theology has only developed weak, ignorant believers who are not ready to give an answer for the cause of Christ. What has caused the demise of the Christian's ability to be ready to share Christ in whatever situation? Some suggest it is due to the plurality of religions present today that were absent years ago in American culture. Others suggest it is the constant barrage of immoral garbage that has stolen the attention of the church. It could also be argued that the constant struggle for political influence for the church has caused many to develop a cynical attitude toward anything religious in nature. All of these seem to be present and a valid part of the discussion.

There is also the notion, however, that we have not prepared ourselves to adequately talk about Jesus—his life, death, resurrection, and ascension and the promise of his return. Again, to some this seems peculiarly simple, but is that not what Paul argues in 1 Corinthians, that the foolishness of God is more than man's attempt at wisdom (1 Cor. 1:25)? In essence, in our misguided wisdom we have decided that the message that changes the world will not work in twenty-first-century America.

We cannot try to argue that salvation works, nor can we try to explain everything about our God. We can only present what he has asked us to proclaim. It is similar to the newspaper editorials that appear in the paper daily. People read the editorials to get the editor's opinion, which is the formal stance of the paper on certain topics of the day. When a Christian speaks, be aware that those who listen perceive it as the "formal stance" of the God we represent. This is the reason God's formal stance is based not on my thoughts, my feelings, or even my relationship to him but rather on Scripture. People do not care what my personal opinion may be, but they need to know God's opinion through Scripture. In order for us to be effective in evangelism, we must get back to presenting Christ and the cross and removing all other barriers.

Paul tells us that the cross of Christ is offensive or a stumbling block, so it should not be considered a surprise when people take offense (1 Cor. 1:18–25).

The cross is offensive because it reveals the heart. Scripture tells us that the heart is deceitful above anything we can imagine (Jer. 17:9). When our heart is under its own authority, it justifies our sin, ignores our prejudices, and excuses our actions. The cross is offensive because it reveals how badly we have skewed the scales in our favor. We condemn other peoples' sin while comforting ourselves that God will understand the sin with which we struggle. When the cross becomes clear in our mind, it reveals that we are in desperate need of a new start.

The cross is offensive because it reveals our deepest struggles. We are a self-made country and do not tend to let others know our weaknesses. It is through the cross that humans are faced with the truth of the need for strength in their life. Paul tells us that through our weakness Christ is made strong (2 Cor. 12:9), which shows us we can only find strength through recognizing our weakness. It is a deep struggle for Americans to admit our need for help. We look at Hollywood, Wall Street, and the Magnificent Mile in Chicago and seem to see happiness, fulfillment, and success. Upon a more intense review, however, we see disappointment, emptiness, and dysfunction that scream for help.

Some people see a changing of the times ahead for American individualism. One survey responder said, "A shift is occurring away from the assumption that the individual is autonomous and complete in and of himself or herself. The conviction is growing that we are part of a larger whole and that our relationship to this larger whole is not fully captured in our relationship to conventional churches and religions." This also seems to suggest that we are embarking on a change in the way people view the cross and the sufficiency of the sacrifice Christ paid.

The cross is offensive because it reveals humans' desire to be in charge. One of our biggest challenges is to submit and let another person lead. Just go on a road trip with another couple or some friends. Everyone wants to be in charge of the radio, the map, the eating plans, the locations to stop, and even planning the entertainment. All of these grabs for power reveal our desire to be in charge. This was first seen in the Garden of Eden. Adam and Eve had everything at their fingertips except one tree. "Do not eat of it" was the command from God, and they could not accept his word. Humans have wanted to be in charge of their own destiny from the beginning, and it ends in destruction. Still today,

150

this is seen in our attempt to find peace and hope apart from Christ—which ends in failure.

Delivering the Message

The keys to our being effective in the future are knowing what we believe and learning how to deliver the message. When creating *The Evangelism Guidebook*, I set out to develop a resource that would enable believers to grow in that second key to effectiveness: learning how to deliver the message of the gospel to distinct people groups across the country. The message of the gospel will not change, as we will discuss later in the chapter, but how we

---

I think evangelism is headed a couple different directions in the next decade. The traditional churches seem to be digging in and going back to methods they have used for decades. The sense is that they used these methods when they were growing and strong, so they need to go back to those methods to be strong again. This will make them effective at reaching a certain group of people who want traditional church or want to feel like they go to a "real church." On the other side, there has been an explosion of new churches of various denominations that are doing church in a way that does not look like church at all. They are reaching people who do not like the boundaries of traditional church. But they are also raising up a generation that is interested in being saved but not always interested in knowing and following God or serving people through a church. Because of these two different issues, personal evangelism will decline as the focus becomes more on churchwide evangelism and event evangelism. There is less emphasis on training people to share their faith and more emphasis on weekly or yearly events to do the evangelism. People are no longer accountable for evangelism; "the church" is responsible for evangelism.

—James Lankford, Baptist General Convention of Oklahoma

---

share the gospel may change based on to whom we are delivering the message. How you share the gospel with a Muslim is different from how you share your faith with a homosexual. With over three hundred pages of expert advice on reaching distinct people groups of our country, *The Evangelism Guidebook* has proven to be a great resource for those who are passionate about sharing their faith. In addition, an online resource has been added to help those who would like to learn how to share their faith with friends. You can access this free resource at www.sharingthefaith. com. This website has thousands of resources for you to use to learn more about sharing your faith effectively.

At this point you may be asking, "How are we to communicate the message of the gospel to a world that is bent on not listening?" All of the survey responders answered our questions with a sense of pessimism about our ability to succeed in seeing this country come to Christ. Yet here is an eye-opening insight: we are called not to bring success but to be faithful. Our task is not in winning or losing but in knowing how to share the plan. The challenge for church leaders today is to focus on training soul winners, not seeing results. Results will come when we know the message and how to communicate it. Every professional coach will tell you that it is a rarity to win or lose a game on the day of the game; usually winning and losing is determined through the process of preparation.

The book *The Apostolic Preaching and Its Development* is a classic on sermon preparation and delivering the gospel. Author C. H. Dodd gives seven key elements to the gospel message:

1. The prophecies are fulfilled, and the new age is inaugurated by the coming of Christ.
2. He was born of the seed of David.
3. He died according to the Scriptures to deliver us out of the present evil age.

4. He was buried.
5. He rose on the third day according to the Scriptures.
6. He is exalted at the right hand of God, as Son of God and Lord of [the] quick and the dead.
7. He will come again as Judge and Savior.[1]

How does this compare to the evangelistic preaching we are hearing today? I used to think evangelism was more about condemning sin than exalting Christ. My early sermons and evangelistic efforts concentrated more on speaking about what I was against than what I was standing for. The gospel does condemn sin, but it does not stop there. I am in favor of communicating the truth that God hates sin and that we are all guilty; however, the main focus of the New Testament is to proclaim the claims of Christ, specifically that God became man. The one attribute of evangelism that is missing from most sermons and evangelistic efforts today is the message that God became one of us. Most religions teach that humans can ultimately become god; Christianity teaches that God became man and walked among us for thirty-three years. Throughout those thirty-three years, Jesus never said, "Pay me" or "Thank me," but he said, "Follow me." Why? Because he knew where he was going. His mission is not to teach, educate, or legislate but to redeem sinners through his sacrifice on the cross.

The term we use for Jesus is the *God-man*. Its meaning isn't clear until we look at Jesus on the cross. It is while he hung on the cross that we see how his deity and humanity intersect: with one outstretched hand, he is completely divine—absolute perfection, God the Son; with the other outstretched hand, he is completely human—taking our sin upon himself. At this pivotal point in history, Jesus became the one who bridged the gap, bringing God and man back together again.

A Superficial Knowledge of God

While I travel, I find what has been reported to us through so many responses: Americans are not ignorant *about* God, but the simple fact is that they do not *know* God. As a whole, the church has done a tremendous job through the centuries in branding the name "Christianity" and being involved in the mainstream of American life. Those days are changing, but for the present there is still a sense of knowing a little about Christianity.

There is evidence, though, that the knowledge is at best superficial. When we asked students at a Bible conference who spoke the words of John 3:16, the most famous verse in the Bible, only a little over half knew it was Jesus. When the question was asked, "Why did Jesus die on the cross?" the answers were shallow at best. "He died for our sins" seemed to be the most prominent response. When we asked why again, we were met mainly with silence. Evidently we as the body of Christ are effective in getting the taglines of our faith intermixed in culture, but the understanding of our message has not reached the masses.

Why did Jesus die on the cross? If we only answer that he died on the cross for our sins, he will never change a person's life. Life change only happens when we take it personally: Jesus died on the cross for *my* sin. *My* pride, lust, greed, jealousy, and other sins placed Jesus on the cross. He did not have to die, due to his innocence, but he loved *me* so much he paid the price for *me*. When that reality takes place in a person's mind and heart, that individual will be forever changed. When it is properly understood, the message of the cross is louder than any noise in the room.

When discussing the role of evangelism and making it informational to our listeners, we should clarify what exactly should be included in the gospel message. Dr. Lewis Drummond, my former teacher and mentor, has written significantly on this topic in his classic work *The Word of the Cross*. He tells us that there are six principles that should be found in all evangelistic proclamations.[2]

1. It begins with the evangelist proclaiming the *incarnation*—God has become man. Again, this is the most overlooked fact that must be presented. We cannot go to God; he came to us.

2. There is also *forgiveness*. Every day we face people who are trying to escape the guilt that enslaves them. The prison doors are opened when the listener hears the forgiveness offered through Christ.

3. We must present *the cross*. As Paul declares in 1 Corinthians 1:23, "We preach Christ crucified." It is our only plea to this world.

4. *Christ has been raised*. Without the resurrection we are all in trouble. We are to be pitied more than anyone else if we are declaring our message and the resurrection did not take place. Josh McDowell's work on the facts of the resurrection is timeless. As a young student who was determined to prove the Bible false, Josh became a Christian when he studied the evidence of the Scriptures. His book *Evidence That Demands a Verdict* is still a bestseller after thirty years. Josh told me, "I could not argue against the existence of God when it was before my face. All the books of history cannot compare to the authenticity of the Scriptures. To doubt the Scriptures would be as foolish as saying that New York does not exist today." Due to the resurrection, we are aware that our faith is not empty, our future is not futile, and our forgiveness is not questioned.

5. The fifth principle is to proclaim *Jesus as the Christ*. *Christ* is the Greek word for *Messiah*. He is the one who was prophesied in the Old Testament and realized in the New Testament.

155

John the Baptist recognizes Jesus as the Christ when he declares, "Behold, the Lamb of God who takes away the sin of the world!" (John 1:29 NASB). When John uses those words, he refers to Isaiah 53 where the Messiah is described as one who would be led like a lamb to the slaughter: "He was oppressed and afflicted, yet he did not open his mouth; he was led like a lamb to the slaughter, and as a sheep before her shearers is silent, so he did not open his mouth" (v. 7). Christ took upon himself our sin. Paul tells us that he who knew no sin became sin for us that we may become the righteousness of God through Jesus Christ (2 Cor. 5:21).

6. The final principle is a *call to repentance*. Acts 2 tells of Peter addressing the crowd with an evangelistic message. At the end of his sermon it is recorded that "when the people heard this, they were cut to the heart and said to Peter and the other apostles, 'Brothers, what shall we do?'" Peter's response is clear: "Repent and be baptized" (vv. 37–38). See this sequence: repent first, then be baptized. Without repentance, there is no genuine conversion. *Repentance* is a translation of the Greek word *metanoia*; it means "a change of direction." Not a change in thought, but a change of being. Repentance is often explained through an illustration of a U-turn of a car, which is simple to understand. But repentance is not only a U-turn, it is stopping the car, getting out of the driver's seat, allowing Christ to get into the driver's seat, and turning the

As the number of evangelism tools and resources increase, the number of people doing evangelism decreases. Ironic!

Currently people believe that our issue is how the gospel is packaged to this culture. But I believe that the challenge is not the packaging of the gospel—the gospel is powerful in any package—it is motivating individuals to share the gospel. I think we as a church have become focused too much on the seed package and not enough on getting people into the field to plant the seeds.

—James Lankford, Baptist General Convention of Oklahoma

car around. Repentance is the point in life where Christ takes over. With this message, how can we remain silent?

As has been revealed, we must make the gospel message informational to the listener, who must translate the message through a barrage of philosophical ideologies that have been presented through every form of media available. The Internet, television, radio, and input from friends bring an unbelievable amount of information that has not been validated. But the cultural shift that has taken place today stresses that if it makes sense, it must be true. That mind-set is dangerous, but it is still the mind-set you will face as you share the message of Christ. In the midst of the information generation, how do we stand apart while sharing the message?

One pastor had an incredible insight about delivering the message: "We only have two options in our opportunities of sharing Christ: (1) We stop sharing; we circle the wagons and prepare for the inevitable. (2) We go forward trusting that he who has called us will be faithful. The battle before us may be one that has insurmountable odds, but like the three Hebrew children, even if he does not save us, we will be found faithful."

A Monopoly on the Market

This really sums up our choices; but how do we stand apart? The message of the gospel is very distinct. It is not something that has been copied. Too often we have tried to copy the world, but what Christ offers is something that cannot be attained from the world: "Peace I leave with you; my peace I give you. I do not give to you as the world gives. Do not let your hearts be troubled and do not be afraid" (John 14:27). What Christ offers is not gained by alcohol, sex, drugs, or anything offered by the world; nothing can compare to the message of the gospel. So since it isn't available here on earth, Christians have a monopoly on the peace market!

The power of a trademark is amazing. If a product can obtain a trademark, it is protected against anything that tries to imitate it. Think of three of the most well-known symbols worldwide: the Olympic rings, Coca-Cola, and the Red Cross. When you see these symbols, you know exactly what they mean and their significance. While I was in Nicaragua on a mission crusade, our team visited a village that had no clean water we could drink. After several hours of intense heat, our water supply was gone. The missionaries told us that although the locals could drink the water, our digestive system would reject the water and result in a condition known to some as "Montezuma's Revenge"—a gastrointestinal nightmare! The team lasted for another hour without water until, finally, we saw the symbol. Not the Olympic rings or the Red Cross (which would have been wonderful), but the waves of Coca-Cola. We knew what it was, and we knew it was safe to drink. In the realm of the spiritual, every believer needs to know the power of Christ's trademark forever!

You should not be intimidated while sharing the gospel. It does need to be informational but not exhaustive. We are all on a journey of faith whether we are brand-new Christians or longtime believers. You should have a goal to improve the knowledge of your faith, like you would do anything else. When anyone starts playing football, they realize it is different from watching it on the television. When people first take dance lessons, they learn firsthand that there is more to it than what is seen by a casual observer.

When you seek to become more aware of evangelistic opportunities, you will discover that each day you study, pray, and listen you will grow in your effectiveness. Share what you do know, and then pray that God will reveal even more to you tomorrow.

11

EVANGELISM STILL WORKS

The Future of Evangelism in America

We are not going to move this world by criticism of it nor conformity to it, but by the combustion within it of lives ignited by the Spirit of God.

—Vance Havner

I am an evangelist. Everything that is conducted within the ministry I lead is about seeing people come to Christ. There were no formulas used in the survey that developed the trends discussed in this book. It was a very simple approach: we asked individuals what they thought would be effective in reaching people with the gospel over the next ten years.

This is not a book about consulting in the arena of evangelism. I am not a consultant. In fact, if I were elected president—though I am not a candidate—the first enactment of Congress would be to outlaw consulting. Consultants are part of the problem we are facing within the church. Most consultants will tell you everything you are doing wrong but not walk with you to get things right.

There are two phrases consultants use that I personally challenge: (1) The definition of *insanity* is doing the same things over and over again and expecting different results. (2) Everything rises and falls on leadership. I suggest that doing the *wrong* things over and over again expecting *right results* is insanity. Doing the *same thing* over and over again is sometimes called *faithfulness*.

Most churches have succumbed to the idea of throwing the baby out with the bathwater in the area of evangelism. We have turned over the idea of reaching the lost with everything from tried-and-true biblical principles to wearing Hawaiian shirts and calling ourselves postmodern experts. I believe we need to put things in perspective. *Postmodernism* is one of the most overused words in our society; everything since 1960 is called *postmodern*. Personally, I wonder what comes after postmodernism—maybe pre-spiritualism? Could we actually be closer to a spiritual renaissance than ever before? People are hungry for something real in the spiritual realm. I challenge anyone who says that evangelism does not work in this culture. I see it in the faces of people in every city I have visited across the country. As people begin to hunt for spiritual satisfaction, the first place they turn is the church. For example, in 2001, after the devastating tragedy in New York, churches were overflowing with people. Some came to pray; others came to find comforting words or an explanation. Both Gallup Poll and Barna Research reported a rise in church attendance immediately following the 9/11 tragedy. In addition, both reported a return to pre-attack attendance within a month.[1] The church obviously missed a pivotal point in history to broadcast a life-changing message to society.

Can we learn from the past and move into the future? I think we can. It is not *if* another tragedy happens, but *when*. The church must position itself to be the voice of biblical reason in society when society asks. People do not care what you are wearing, how cool the platform is, or how many plasma screens the church has on the wall. People desire to have real biblical answers for their situation.

Contrary to this first popular catchphrase of consultants—the definition of *insanity* is doing the same thing repeatedly and expecting different results—sometimes we must expect different results when we are faithful in doing the same things over and over again. The gospel must be shared with a person repeatedly, in various ways and means, in hopes of that person eventually coming to Christ. Invitations from the platform are given time and again, even though some may not respond immediately. From the very practical aspect of everyday life, a parent consistently teaches a young child in hopes that the toddler will eventually learn obedience. Rather than *insanity*, it is *faithfulness* to do the same thing over and over again and expect different results.

The other day I was busy with a project for my home. It was a hot day, and I'm not the most domesticated husband. This project was in need of a handyman—someone who knew what to do and didn't mind doing the work. I called and arranged an appointment with a handyman. When he arrived to start work, he assured me he could handle the project but that the cost was going to be considerably more than he had originally thought. The reason for this increase was due to my incompetence; I had actually torn up another piece of the roof when I was trying to do the project myself. Here is the reality for evangelism with the church. We know the answer for everyone's life is found in Christ, but sometimes people have to mess up their lives to realize the need. Of course this is in

161

regard to evangelism, not spiritual growth. This is a book not about church growth but about seeing people come to Christ. Continue the programs, building campaigns, and any other aspect of church growth you feel is necessary, but when the time arises to address your community about Jesus Christ, do not be unprepared.

The second phrase of consultants that I challenge is that "everything rises and falls on leadership." That is not necessarily the case—everything rises and falls on *lordship*. We must train ourselves to be men and women of God, not well-dressed executives. A pastor friend of mine said this reality struck him when he looked on his shelf and saw that the books on leadership were growing and the books on the Holy Spirit were shrinking. We must live to be balanced in the Christian life. We must be not only leaders but *godly* leaders.

I want you to understand that if you disagree with the principles in this book your argument is not with me. These issues were developed by thousands of interviews and surveys that were answered by people like you: students, adults, clergy, laypeople, ministers, homemakers, and businesspeople. In closing, I would like to include a sampling of responses from people around the country who have answered the question,

---

I have found that evangelism in our generation, in Southern California and surely in the Hollywood entertainment industry, is only effective if we as Christians are vulnerable, honest, and open and if we truly care about the individual we're talking to. We can't state enough facts to convince anyone of the existence of Jesus, but we can tell about what we have experienced, what we have discovered, and what we know has changed us. And if we tell stories about how we have had encounters with Jesus, then that is even more powerful.

The unbelievers in my world are hungry for affirmation and love. They don't want to be told what to do or how to act. They want to be told that they have value, and they want to hear life-changing stories that others have experienced. Then we have their attention.

—Karen Covell, TV producer; Hollywood Prayer Network

I encourage Christians in my world to take time to *ask people questions*, find out what makes them tick, and discover what they are passionate about. Then the Christian can transition into personal stories that relate to their journey. One of the best ways to start a powerful conversation about God is to ask what their relationship with their father is. When people start to open up about their father, they will reveal what their relationship to God probably is. And the passion toward or against their father will tell the believer what needs to happen to help the unbeliever be more open to God. The two relationships are very tied together for all people, whether they realize it or not.

So we can't necessarily use the "Four Spiritual Laws" or be armed with all the latest apologetics. But we can tell stories, ask questions, and build personal relationships with the people God has put on our heart or placed in our path.

—Karen Covell, TV producer; Hollywood Prayer Network

"What do we need to do to be effective in reaching this next generation?"

As you read these responses, it is my prayer that something inside of you will resonate with a burning passion to share Christ. May our one desire in life be to be found faithful in Christ. Carry on! The world is dying to hear the message of the gospel.

REACHING THE NEXT GENERATION?

Thoughts on the Future of Evangelism from Ministry Leaders

Cliff Barrows
Program Director, Billy Graham Evangelistic Association

"There will always be a need for evangelism. The lost will always be with us. Large mass meetings may be more difficult than in the past unless targeted toward youth in a cutting-edge way. Individuals will have to step up with one-on-one/workplace evangelism as described by Joe Aldrich in *Lifestyle Evangelism*. Individuals will have to serve as ambassadors for Christ who can explain the gospel out of conviction."

Rick Marshall
Former Director of Crusades and Follow-Up, Billy Graham Evangelistic Association

"Evangelism will be based not on what we are doing but on who we are. The world is watching. Ministry foundations will be laid by character and integrity. Recent surveys show that Christianity the religion is 'out' but the person of Jesus is 'in.' We must get rid of all stumbling blocks, except the cross, to someone coming to have a personal relationship with Christ. We must be cautious not to lose spiritual authority for the sake of relevancy. Going to natural gathering places and events will provide good opportunities for evangelism."

Tom Phillips
Vice President, Billy Graham Evangelistic Association

"I believe evangelism is going to the common men and women, especially in whatever their workplace is, including the home. The first reformation took the Word of God to the common man. The second reformation will take the work and the Word of God to those and other locations."

Art Bailey
Festival Director, Franklin Graham Festivals

"First: Evangelism will continue to move into the relational realm. What I see coming will be organizations providing opportunity for individuals to reach out to their peers. Proclamation organizations as well as churches will continue to be perceived as impersonal to the unchurched but will play a vital role in aiding the body in keeping evangelism primary.

"Second: In order to sustain itself the church will turn more and more to true discipleship. Not necessarily to what it has called discipleship but to a neo-teric paradigm that calls for a deeper commitment to reproduction of converts. This new paradigm will, I think, bring some sort of purging among evangelicals driving the uncommitted to groups that do not focus on these basics.

"Third: Research will become more important to evangelism. We, as organizations, will need to become more aware of how our target audience relates to our message and our delivery technique. This does not mean compromising the spiritual element of our system or necessarily changing the look. It does mean that as we increasingly face audiences that demand to know 'what's in it for me?' we certainly will need to begin to apply the message toward the felt need of unbelievers."

Jeff Anderson
Billy Graham Crusade Director

"Effective evangelism is relational. It is relating to individuals one-on-one. It is intentionally being there at a point of need to comfort and encourage in practical ways. It is letting people you are praying for see that you have needs and letting them help you. For example: Our dryer went out and five loads of clothes needed to be dried, so off to the neighbors we went. They are a family we have been praying for, and our request for the use of their dryer was received with open arms. Or, we asked neighbors down the block, whom we had not formally met, for the use of their pool following our son's wedding rehearsal because he and his bride-to-be wanted to be baptized prior to being married the next day. Needs and brokenness open avenues to share the love of Christ in practical ways that can lead to a clear presentation of the gospel. And we as Christ-followers always need to be

167

prepared to share the reason for the hope that we have in our lives with gentleness and respect."

David Bruce
Vice President, Billy Graham Evangelistic Association
"I believe that the most effective evangelism for the next decade will occur out of creative partnering between ministries. The ability to 'cross touch' between existing groups for more focused and energized approaches will be exciting. Of course continued emphasis on lifestyle evangelism within church ministries and outreaches will also continue to maximize the church's influence in the community."

Jay Strack
President, Student Leadership University, Orlando, Florida
"Relational evangelism must be stressed. People need to be touched before they will listen. This generation wants to see your faith before they hear your message."

Karl Overbeek
Regional Strategist, Central California Classis, Reformed Church in America, Sacramento, California
Speaker, BGEA Schools of Evangelism
"I believe there will always be crusades of various types meeting different cultural needs and desires. But I'm not necessarily convinced this is or will be the most effective. I sense there is an apostolic movement around the world that is focused on church planting. There is sufficient evidence that the conversion curve goes up significantly in church planting. I see this as one of the more personal and long-lasting ways of getting people into the kingdom and discipled to become evangelists. I also sense that evangelism is calling people to a personal

relationship with Jesus Christ and not so much to the organized church, because of all the baggage associated with the church."

Michael Guido
Pursuing Relationship Ministries, Franklin, Tennessee
Road Chaplain to Christian Bands

"I believe that the future to evangelism in the next decade will be to invade the culture in a relevant way. To reach this hurting and angry generation of youth, they need to see and hear a message that is relevant to their times. I believe that evangelism is moving through the arts and entertainment and not in a structured format. You must plant new seed in the field dedicated for the new harvest—last season's crop has already been harvested and there is a new fresh crop waiting. Jeremiah 33:3: 'Call to me and I will answer you and tell you great and unsearchable things you do not know.'"

Jonathan Lenning
Bible Study Leader, Freshman, University of Alabama

"Less and less will effective evangelism be administered by a few well-known faces. Rather, the gospel will be shared through the hundreds of millions of faces that comprise the body of Christ. This means that our heart, vision, and love must replace the hypocrisy of condescending, self-righteous judgment within the church. We, his body, have to carry out our original purpose by making disciples, not merely converts. Satisfaction must cease as we thirst for more and, in unreserved faith, expect more. God will give us his grace in prayer, for God honors sincere prayer. And as the people of the church awaken to the power and presence of the Holy Spirit within them, true evangelism will inevitably follow."

C. G. Maclin
Vice President, Marketplace Chaplains, Dallas, Texas

"Reaching the lost through the workplace by building relationships through service to the employees and individuals will earn their trust and the right to share our faith."

Larry Backlund
Former Director, BGEA School of Evangelism, Minneapolis, Minnesota

"I think there is a renewed emphasis on evangelism throughout all denominations and countries. Having just been to Egypt, Israel, and Holland, I think some of the other countries put us to shame. There is a real heart to reach out to people even though it means persecution. I sometimes wonder if it isn't even *because* of persecution!

"In Egypt, one of the most repressive countries as far as Christians are concerned, the Christians there are very bold in their faith even though they know it may even mean *persecution* and *prison*. On the other hand, in Holland there is no persecution, but there is also very little outreach."

Dan Southern
Former President, American Tract Society, Dallas, Texas

"I think those who do evangelism will need to become more and more skilled at connecting the gospel relevantly to what is going on in the world and less focused on just telling people that it is the right thing to have a relationship with God. We will need to give evangelizers good tools to do that, and training will be important in that effort. There won't be any Billy Grahams or James Kennedys to do it for us—so there will be more specialization

170

needed that focuses on various forms of evangelization. There will be more and more charismatics and extreme fundamentalists in the forefront of Christianity, and this may be a turnoff to the secular mind. Bigger churches with 'successful programs' will be the norm, but they will do very little real evangelism. Partnerships among serious evangelical ministries will be essential to the success of spreading the Christian message. Most evangelism will be to the developing world, that is to say, to an international audience and maybe within the military."

Anthony Jordan
Former Director, Baptist General Conference of Oklahoma

"Local church evangelists in America are an endangered species. Toward the end of the twentieth century the traditional revival and evangelistic meeting in local churches that utilized an evangelist began to fall out of favor. Now only a small percentage use these methods. Evangelistic events using a myriad of methods have replaced them. This occurred in the cities first, and now I see it happening in the rural areas as well."

Ellis Brust
President, The Anglican Mission in America, Pawleys Island, South Carolina

"I'll give you my impressions formed from observation, direct contact, and twenty-five years of having watched the church rather closely as it implodes on itself in the West and prospers in the global South. I offer five major thoughts about Christian evangelism at the beginning of the twenty-first century.

1. The missional influence of the global South: Africa, South America, and Asia have clearly been anointed

171

by God for the greatest evangelical movement in the twenty-first century. For example: The Anglican church in particular, which was so heavily influenced by the East Africa revival, has played a significant role in new missionary initiatives in the west. Rwanda, Kenya, Uganda, and Nigeria in Western Africa have all experienced significant growth in the numbers of new Christian converts. They are now assisting in missionary initiatives in the Americas and Europe. We can expect to see more mission efforts from the global South in the next one hundred years, particularly from Africa, South America, and Asia.

2. Crisis of faith and crisis of leadership: The revisionist theological and moral issues facing the Episcopal Church will spill over into all other American denominations to one degree or another. The failure of the leaders of the 'old mainline' denominations to correct theological drift away from historic Christianity will cause a huge exodus from these denominations if leaders fail to act. There will be a rise in authentic evangelical partnerships that are able to cross cultural, denominational, and geographic boundaries effectively. Those denominations or ministries that choose to go it alone will likely lose effectiveness and may decline. Theological clarity coupled with partnership and mission-driven leadership will open the door to the greatest evangelistic efforts in the next century.

3. Ancient-Future: Megachurches are (with notable exceptions) a U.S. movement of God. Yet worldwide, the greatest evangelism and growth in Christianity will be in the ancient liturgical churches in the global South. Nigeria currently has 18 million Anglicans and has set in motion plans to double that number in three to

five years. The Anglican Church in Uganda will double from 9 to 18 million in the same time frame. Clearly, God is using these churches with historic liturgies and customs, and we need to ask what this says to North American and Western Christianity.

4. Governmental influence: I believe there will be a serious attempt to tax church properties and to remove some (if not all) church-related charitable tax deductions in the next ten years. The church should be prepared for this political move. If these attempts to tax churches fall short, there may be significant strings attached to churches' tax-exempt status.

5. Islam: The clear 'right and wrong' teaching of Islam will become increasingly attractive to youth in North America and throughout Western culture. The government will adjust itself more and more to accommodate Islam. The church will, for the first time in U.S. history, find itself trying to evangelize in an increasingly pluralistic society and presenting the gospel as one alternative to Islam. We better study history to work through the evangelistic challenges we will face. Clarity of vision and values, not appeasement, is the lesson of history."

James Lankford
Director of Youth, Baptist General Conference of Oklahoma, Falls Creek

"I think evangelism is headed a couple different ways in the next decade. The traditional churches seem to be digging in and going back to holding revivals and doing what they have done well for fifty years. They will be effective at reaching a certain group of people who want traditional church or want to feel like they go to a 'real church.' On the other side, there has been an explosion of new churches of

173

various denominations that are doing church in a way that does not look like church at all. They are reaching people who do not like the boundaries of church. But they are also raising up a generation that is interested in being saved but not always interested in knowing and following God. Along with that, personal evangelism will decline as more church evangelism increases. There is less emphasis on training people to share their faith and more emphasis on weekly or yearly events to do the evangelism.

"As the number of evangelism tools and resources increase, the number of people doing evangelism decreases. Ironic. I know that may seem pessimistic, but I do not intend for it to be that way. The challenge is not the packaging of the gospel—the gospel is powerful in any package because it motivates individuals to share their faith. I think we as a church have become focused too much on the seed package and not enough on getting people into the field to plant the seed."

Thoughts on the Future of Evangelism from Businesspeople

Johnson Ellis
President, CURA Emergency Services, Dallas, Texas
Amazon Outreach, Founding Board Member and Former Board Chaplain

"Evangelism is headed outside of the walls of the church. If a church is only content to reach those that feel safe enough to come inside their walls, that church could very well die. You can take a course practically every week to learn a different way to share the gospel. The lost world is not looking for another fancy presentation—it is looking for hope and a genuine individual sharing the simple message."

Kirk Humphries
Former Mayor of Oklahoma City, Oklahoma
Candidate for U.S. Senate

"Evangelism in the next decade will be very much in the context of a secular society. We live in a society in which most people do not know God as Creator and Father—they believe in 'god' but do not *know God.*

"Effective evangelism will be any method that communicates the truth of God's love through Jesus Christ so that needy, hurting people can understand it. That will tend to be out in the marketplace through music and seminars that deal with areas of need in their lives—any way to reach people where they are, because most of them are not going to walk into a traditional church.

"I think we're back to Andrew bringing his brother to meet Jesus. Jesus met Simon down on the lakeshore, not at the synagogue. So this is nothing new. But we will have to continually adapt our delivery so that we tear down barriers and reach out to people where they are living.

"We must reach people on their own turf, using their language without our 'churchy' forms of language. People will respond to individuals who show them some personal interest, a listening attitude, and love. People are particularly interested in listening to your spiritual message if you have reached out to touch them in their areas of physical and emotional need."

Chris Mechsner
President, Ascendio Computer Company, Dallas, Texas

"Change is imperative, yet not in the truths of Scripture but rather in the tone, manner, and importance of the message being delivered. Evangelism is for the lost, except the lost don't realize they are lost. Technology, sex, liquor, priorities, and so forth have all temporarily

175

filled the voids of lost hearts. We need to show the lost why they are lost. The tough part is 'catching' the lost to do this. How do you accomplish this in a free-will, do-what-you-want America? Evangelism over the coming years will not only address this issue but raise up solutions from leaders present and leaders yet to be named. Evangelism could be the next American revolution ... taking us back to a civilization focused on Christ, family, love, and truth ... away from the lies we are fed daily, ... which the lost have come to know as truth."

Larry Collette
President, Cass Bank, St. Louis, Missouri

"The answer to your question depends on whether you meant the geographical direction evangelism is taking or the intrinsic nature of the activity itself. If you mean the former, it is my understanding that the direction is strongly toward Asia and then Africa. They seem to be ripe for significant growth in Christianity.

"If, however, you meant the activity itself, I think it depends on whether you mean successful evangelism or activity-based evangelism. By activity-based, I mean the kind of evangelism that teaches a certain number of steps to take or the application of a formula to convince someone to accept Christ. I think the effectiveness of this form will continue to diminish and more successful evangelism will be relationally based and will impact the culture more. While there will always be a need for large events to present the gospel, it will be the modeling and mentoring of the Christian life view that will draw people to Christ."

Barbara Green
Co-Owner, Buyer, Hobby Lobby, Oklahoma City, Oklahoma

"I believe, sad to say, that a lot of our churches are not reaching the lost here in the U.S. They are compromising the message and also the time the church doors are open for corporate worship.

"Crusades and large gatherings of people from all denominations coming together, such as Promise Keepers, seem to be a good tool of evangelism. Also, it seems that the message of Christ being taught to the homeless is a very viable tool of evangelism. Since I am involved in working with the homeless here in Oklahoma City, I know they have open hearts and needs for the Word of God. They are at the bottom and are desperate for the hope of our resurrected Christ. Also, their numbers are increasing each year. It is a great problem in our society today."

Ed Martin
President, Ackerman-McQueen Advertising
Former GM Oklahoman

"Here is my take on evangelism in the coming years. I feel the direction of evangelism will head more toward one-on-one lifestyle contact. If I as a believer come alongside an unbeliever, my friendship and concern for the person puts me in a good position to share the gospel with him or her. I think the church will always have its place in evangelism, but I am convinced that personal contact is the direction we will see more and more. Best advertising is still word-of-mouth."

Larry Ross
President, A. Larry Ross and Associates (public relations/media relations), Dallas, Texas

"Marquee Christian leaders with the gift of evangelism are still holding citywide crusades (e.g., Billy Graham and Luis Palau). But many ministries are using a more niche-oriented method for taking the gospel to the marketplace, mirroring businesses such as Peter Lowe Success Semi-

177

nars. This includes organizations and individuals trying to reach the next generation, which statistics show remain outside the grasp of the church but who continue to respond well to the body life concept—combining music and extreme sports with a gospel message that is still relevant to them.

"I think Rick Warren is onto something when he says we are on the verge of a new reformation. Like the first in Martin Luther's day, we are experiencing a polarization of our culture. But if the first reformation was about belief, the next will be about behavior—as the church puts legs on its faith. Pastor Rick has said that the Bible refers to the church as the 'body of Christ,' but we have lost our hands and arms and have been reduced to a mouth. While preaching is necessary, we need to get out of the pew and start *being* the church, taking care of the disfranchised and so forth. Promise Keepers is modeling this by challenging men to get out of the arenas and into the marketplace and engage the culture with a biblical worldview.

"Also, when you look at the impact of *The Passion of the Christ*, that and other faith and family films have made the gospel unavoidable in our culture. I believe that movies, emerging media, and the arts will be part of the new wave of evangelism as we leverage the power of story to convey the ultimate story of redemption through the life-changing message of the gospel."

Thoughts on the Future of Evangelism from Pastors and Youth Leaders

"The 'extras' beyond the message become increasingly the center of what draws people. Your average non-Christian is not going to come to a 'so-and-so crusade,' but they will come to a high-quality, edgy event." *Michael, Pulse Ministries*

"Evangelism will need to be a big variety—lots of noninstitutional, Christ-centered assemblies in homes, parks, and streets. Special events and invitations are part of 'life sharing.'" *Bob B.*

"Community service will be used as a tool for evangelism. Neighborhood outreach through identifying needs and meeting them and similar outreach methods will gain a greater hearing for the gospel." *Dave P.*

"Evangelism will move more toward entertaining than evangelizing. I say that as a caution that we do not let the message become watered down. Beyond that, I believe that evangelism will be more lifestyle evangelism." *Joe M., Acts International*

"Evangelism will move more outside the church—focused on events more than today. Possibly it will be less toward mass media and more toward niche ministries. There will be a continued strong role of music, but more in the mainstream sense, that is, the 'crossover' trend will mature and become mainstream." *James O., Shout Student Ministries*

"Evangelism will move away from the institutional event to a missional focus of engagement in the marketplace and culture in which we find ourselves." *Rick M., Portland*

"As a woman, I love watching God open venues for women. This is the emerging generation. I'm from the boomer generation, and I'm looking for opportunities to open my mind—thinking outside the box. Relationships are big, and I want to hear what this generation is doing." *Connie, Home Ministries*

179

"Evangelism will be going to public places, parks, malls, sporting events, and so forth." *Harry D.*

"Evangelism will be more about equipping all people to be evangelists—sent out as agents in God's mission in the world. Evangelism will be less 'clergy centered,' more relationship driven, and more Spirit filled. It will be by capturing and captivating people with an urgency for the gospel." *Jen N.*

"Evangelism will be done in home studies, community events (probably seasonal at the church), and servant evangelism." *Dick O.*

"Evangelism will be through churches involved in community work projects such as cleaning up public schools and doing other community projects as a preliminary platform for sharing the gospel through developing relationships with leaders and people in the community." *Fred H.*

"Evangelism will be 'less show' and more 'go.' Evangelism at a personal level, where Christians aren't expected to go . . . being more relevant and showing the excellence of a life lived with Christ." *Jonathan B.*

"People are looking for an understanding of the true gospel, not a water-downed version. It must be complete in both message (1 Cor. 15) and lifestyle of presenter." *Jason M., Trussville*

"Eventually evangelism will be characterized as a hate crime. Before we can blink, we will see pastors and church members in jail for sharing the Good News. Then it will be too late to let our voices be heard." *David, Boaz*

"For effective evangelism, the church will have to first become a greater servant to the community." *Andrew, Brasstown*

"We will discover that 'build it and they will come' only works in the *Field of Dreams*." *Jerry, Warrior*

"Evangelism will be through service, acts of kindness, and undeserved love." *Matt, Vinemont*

"Evangelism will happen by mobilizing the church to serve the community and strengthening the families within the church to reflect Christ's love for the church. Even the lost want a family that works. It will attract the world's attention and open doors for us to share with our neighbors." *Reagan, McDonough*

"Evangelism will happen through service. . . . An example would be a banquet for prostitutes hosted by the church or joining with another group in the AIDS fight." *Brent, Orlando*

"The most effective evangelism today is through personal encounters, not crusades. Prayer is the foundation. Churches need to be united. God's people need to be able to demonstrate the power of God in evangelism." *Dave, Dothan*

"Some of the best opportunities to engage lost people are meeting physical needs and then meeting their spiritual needs. It is when the church takes on the 'it's not about me' mentality that we actually begin to do something radical for God." *Kenneth, Lexington*

"Door-to-door evangelism has gone by the wayside for the most part. Relationship evangelism, use of tracts at businesses, and less confrontational methods are sought. The local church is dependent on how much the pastor is evangelistic. More and more churches today are becoming less evangelistic, and this explains why the church is not growing." *Jeremy, Oklahoma*

"In the emerging church, kids want lives of significance. They are spiritually hungry, more educated, and less tolerant of hypocritical pseudo-Christians." *Jason, Virgina*

"I think we will see a greater decline in evangelism due to lack of liberty and freedom as well as general lack of concern for other people's souls. I don't think it is intentional, but it seems everybody gets too busy and wrapped up in their own lives." *Shelley, Ohio*

"Programs run a mile long but are only an inch deep. Until we reach parents, we are just running up numbers on how many youth have been reached. Commitment is shallow and lasts only until someone else comes along to entertain them." *Phillip, Hanceville*

"I see parachurch groups becoming more effective in our community because people actually see lives being changed by action and people being helped rather than judged or condemned by the religious crowd." *Tim, Virginia*

"I am sensing an increased need in providing opportunities for people to come and ask questions in a nonthreatening environment." *Todd, Lancaster*

"I am sensing a trend in evangelism toward reaching out through apartment ministries, workplace ministries, and meeting physical needs." *Larry, South Carolina*

"We have got to take it to them; they are not coming to us." *John, Georgia*

"People are more concerned and deliberate about connecting with others, developing relationships, and leading others to Christ—no more just sharing truth, but truth and grace." *Andy, Birmingham*

"Relationships—they have to know that you genuinely care about them and what they are dealing with in their lives. They can't just be a number." *Gay, Tennessee*

"Evangelism is about loving them, building relationships, and meeting needs in our community. We are currently searching for what our niche is to reach people in our community. We are great at going and reaching people in other parts of the city, state, and country, but we are not reaching people in our own surrounding community." *Susanne, South Carolina*

"Relationships: The key to this generation is not the flash-in-the-pan programming or even great preaching. They really just want to know that someone is interested in their lives and will invest in their lives long-term. It has to be real. People have to see the wonderful change that Jesus makes in our lives." *Keith, Alabama*

"We have to stop coming across as against stuff and show them what we are for." *Bryan, Georgia*

FREE ONLINE RESOURCES

www.sharingthefaith.com
- Seekers can learn about the gospel of Jesus Christ, review testimonies of believers, and find answers to hard questions about salvation.
- Believers can learn how to witness and use the Testimony Builder to share their faith through an interactive online experience.
- Seekers and believers can find a comprehensive calendar of upcoming seminars, festivals, and crusades.

www.scottdawson.org
- Discover ways to partner with SDEA through prayer, giving, or volunteering.
- Find a comprehensive calendar of upcoming seminars, festivals, and crusades.
- Discover more about the history and mission of SDEA.

www.safeathomeministries.org
- Visit this site to find more information regarding the SDEA Safe at Home ministry, view the upcoming schedule, and discover ways to participate.

www.strengthtostand.com

- This site provides more information regarding the SDEA Student Strength to Stand Conferences, the upcoming schedule, and featured speakers and artists.

www.thepowerofoneconference.com

- Visit this site to find more information regarding the SDEA Senior Adult Conferences, view the upcoming schedule, and learn more about featured speakers and artists.

NOTES

Introduction

1. *Christianity Today*, "Just As We Were: Is Mass Evangelism Dead?" July 5, 2007.

Chapter 1 Lost in the Shuffle

1. Sermon by John Piper, pastor, Bethlehem Baptist Church, Minneapolis, MN, November 14, 1982.

2. Kenneth S. Kantzer and Carl F. H. Henry, eds., *Evangelical Affirmations* (Grand Rapids: Academie Books, 1990), 30.

3. Josh D. McDowell, *Right from Wrong* (Nashville: Nelson, 1994), 245–47.

4. Ibid., 247–48.

Chapter 2 Own Up

1. Phil Cooke, "Is Authenticity as Rare as It Seems for Pastors and Non-Profit Leaders?" *The Change Revolution*, October 11, 2007, www.philcooke.com/authenticity_questions.

2. Adapted from David Edwards, *Lit: Living Christ's Character from the Inside Out* (West Monroe, LA: Howard Publishing, 2002), 114–19.

3. Pat Williams, "Integrity Is King," *Souls of Steel: How to Build Character in Ourselves and Our Kids* (New York: FaithWords, 2008).

4. Henry G. Brinton, "Do-It-Yourself Christianity," Opinion Column, *USA Today*, October 29, 2007, http://blogs.usatoday.com/oped/2007/10/do-it-yourself.html. Brinton is pastor of Fairfax Presbyterian Church in Virginia and author of *Balancing Acts: Obligation, Liberation, and Contemporary Christian Conflicts* (Lima, OH: CSS, 2006).

5. Pat Williams, "Integrity Is King," *New Man Magazine*, November–December 2007, http://www.newmanmagazine.com/display.php?id=16117.

Chapter 3 Listen Up

1. Josh McDowell, phone conversation with David Sanford, February 14, 2003.

Chapter 6 Ready and Willing

1. Oswald Chambers, *My Utmost for His Highest* (Grand Rapids: Discovery House, 1992), January 26.

2. *Christianity Today*, online interview, May 1, 2006, www.ctlibrary.com/ct/2006/may/23.40.html.

Chapter 7 Improve the Process

1. "Just As We Were: Is Mass Evangelism Dead?" *Christianity Today*, July 5, 2007, www.christianitytoday.com/ct/2007/july/11.54.html.

2. "The Progressive Politics of the Millennial Generation," New Politics Institute, June 20, 2007, http://www.newpolitics.net/node/360.

3. "Sticky but Useful Mistakes," Oracle Thinkquest Education Foundation, 2001, http://library.thinkquest.org/J0112389/sticky_but_useful_mistakes.htm.

4. John C. Maxwell, *The 21 Irrefutable Laws of Leadership: Follow Them and People Will Follow You*, Tenth Anniversary Edition (Nashville: Thomas Nelson, 2007), 1–5.

Chapter 8 The Christian Bubble

1. http://www.tentmaker.org/Quotes/evangelismquotes.htm.

Chapter 9 No Lone Rangers

1. Tony Evans, *America's Only Hope* (Chicago: Moody Press, 1990), 109.

Chapter 10 Nothing but the Cross

1. C. H. Dodd, *The Apostolic Preaching and Its Developments: Three Lectures* (Chicago: Willett, Clark and Company, 1937).

2. Lewis A. Drummond, *The Word of the Cross: A Contemporary Theology of Evangelism* (Nashville: Broadman, 1992).

Chapter 11 Evangelism Still Works

1. Laurie Goodstein, "A Nation Challenged: Religion; As Attacks' Impact Recedes, A Return to Religion as Usual," *New York Times*, November 26, 2001, http://query.nytimes.com/gst/fullpage.html?res=9900E3DD113AF935A15752C1A9679C8B63.

ABOUT THE AUTHOR

Scott Dawson has taken to heart the words of Jesus in Matthew 28 when he commissioned his disciples to "go and make disciples of all nations, baptizing them in the name of the Father and of the Son and of the Holy Spirit" (v. 19).

As founder of the Scott Dawson Evangelistic Association (SDEA), Scott has shared the gospel face-to-face with more than one million people since the start of SDEA in 1987. The organization participates in crusades and hosts student and adult conferences, revivals, and other evangelistic outreaches. SDEA does all of this with the mission, "To be innovative and evangelistic by proclaiming the gospel, producing disciples, and partnering with Christian leaders."

An innovative outreach tool used by SDEA is its Safe at Home events, which are in partnership with minor league baseball teams. Through this program, Scott has the opportunity to annually address over 100,000 people in ballparks across the country.

Scott committed his life to Christ at an early age and began preaching the gospel as a teenager. From his youth, the Lord placed a burden on him to share his faith.

In 1989 he earned his bachelor of arts degree in religion and minor in speech at Samford University in Birmingham, Alabama. Samford's campus houses Beeson Divinity School, which is where Scott received his Master of Divinity in 1993. As a student at Beeson, he had the distinct opportunity to serve as Dr. Lewis Drummond's fellow for the Billy Graham Chair of Evangelism. He recently received an honorary doctorate from Covington Theological Seminary.

Scott's Christian ministry extends past SDEA and encompasses the world. He is one of nine evangelists who make up the Next Generation Alliance (NGA), which is a strategic partnership with the Luis Palau Evangelistic Association. Scott is also involved with international missions in Third World countries and has started summer missions programs for students to work in the United States.

In addition to *Evangelism Today*, Scott is the author of *The Complete Evangelism Guidebook: Expert Advice on Reaching Others for Christ, Dear Lord Why? Finding Answers to Life's Most Challenging Questions, The Peace That Can Pass the Pressure Test*, and *The Exchanged Life*. Scott lives with his wife, Tarra, son, Hunter, and daughter, Hope, in his hometown of Birmingham, Alabama, where SDEA's headquarters is located.

Scott Dawson
Scott Dawson Evangelistic Association
400 Office Park Drive, Suite 150
Birmingham, Alabama 35223
(205) 833-9163
sdawson@scottdawson.org

ALSO BY SCOTT DAWSON

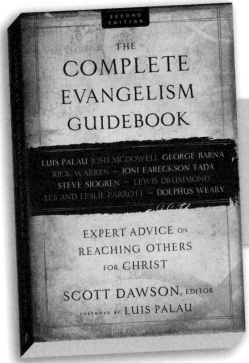

The Complete
Evangelism Guidebook:
Expert Advice on Reaching
Others for Christ

Scott Dawson, editor

9780801066153
400 pp. · $16.99p

Nearly ten million Americans have recently said they are "absolutely committed" to both the Christian faith and to sharing the Good News of Jesus Christ with others. Still, many people don't know where to start, what to say, or how to say it.

The Complete Evangelism Guidebook is a comprehensive resource on everything people need to know about sharing their faith. Well-known evangelists such as Rick Warren, Josh McDowell, and Luis Palau combine their knowledge into one comprehensive and easy-to-read handbook. The insight in this applicable guide will explain how to define, demonstrate, declare, and defend faith with almost anyone from almost any background—whether it's a friend, co-worker, atheist, agnostic, or someone else.

"Scott Dawson and his friends have masterfully crafted a comprehensive guide that is sure to be a practical tool in the workshop of the mind, to be consulted often for evangelistic excellence."

—**John Corts, former president of the Billy Graham Evangelistic Association**

BakerBooks
a division of Baker Publishing Group
www.BakerBooks.com